What's Behind the Smile?

My Journey with Bipolar Disorder

Nancy McCurdy Montagna

I have tried to recreate events, locales and conversations from my memories of them. In order to maintain their anonymity in some instances I have changed the names of individuals, places, and identifying details have been changed to protect the privacy of individuals.

What's Behind the Smile?: My Journey with Bipolar Disorder
Copyright © 2019 Nancy McCurdy Montagna. All rights reserved.

First edition, December 2013
Second edition, September 2016
Third edition, July 2019

This book represents the personal opinions of the author and in no way reflects the views or opinions of any other party, including **Help Network of Northeast Ohio** (formerly called **Help Hotline Crisis Center, Inc.** as called throughout this book).

Montagna, Nancy McCurdy
What's Behind the Smile. My Journey with Bipolar Disorder.
CreateSpace, 2013 **(Createspace now under Kindle Direct Publishing, 2019)** 204p

1. Mental Health - Personal Narrative. 2. Bipolar Disorder

616.0895
ISBN: 9781494350109

Published in the United States of America.
Website: www.whatsbehindthesmile.com

Contents

ACKNOWLEDGEMENTS

I want to thank my family: my parents, Joan and Stewart McCurdy, my three sisters, Chris Brown, Virginia (Gini) Stevenson, Linda Liebermann, and my brother-in-law, Keith Brown who have all encouraged me and helped me through the worst storms of depression and mania.

I am especially thankful for my husband Gary. Words cannot express how you have enriched my life, shown me unconditional love and support, and most of all, you've helped me stay stable. I am so very happy to have you to grow old with!

I would also like to thank the Help Network of Northeast Ohio (formerly named Help Hotline Crisis Center, Inc.) and Coleman Professional Services for employing me—not despite of, but *because of* my recovery from mental illness.

Many thanks to Pan Sankey for editing, Neb (Ben) Brown for the cover graphic design and a big shout-out to Marketing Resources and Results, Inc. for proofing and formatting.

I would like to dedicate this book to my six nieces and nephews. It has been my prayer that none of them suffer with mental illness. I pray that the gene that caused this illness not be handed down to any of them, and so far God has been gracious to answer that prayer.

My nieces and nephews mean more to me than they could ever know, and I pray for them daily:

Justin Liebermann
Vince Liebermann
Benjamin (Neb) Brown
Rebecca Brown
Theodore (Ted) Livingstine
Paige Stevenson

I would like to thank every person that I met throughout my journey who gave me a kind word when I truly needed it. There are too many people to mention.

INTRODUCTION

Why did I decide to write a book telling my inmost secrets of dealing with a mental illness? My first reason is to help others: those whom I have met or have yet to meet who **suffer** with mental illness and/or substance abuse addictions on a daily basis. You know who you are! I call people who have been diagnosed with mental illness my brothers and sisters. We have a kinship. I truly love all of you! My goal is to assist anyone dealing with these issues to learn to master your mind. Hence the reason that my support group, MasterMinds: Be the Master of Your Own, was formed.

There has been a real shift over the years when it comes to mental health that needs to be addressed. The widespread evidences of mental illness are becoming epidemic as more and more psychiatric hospital units are closing due to lack of funds. Although it costs tax payers much more to house a person in jail or prison! Is it really fair for an individual to be sitting in jail when all he/she really needs is some compassion and the right psychotropic medication?

This book was also written to shine some light on that misunderstood word: suicide. Suicide is something that needs to be talked about. The wounds to family members left behind from such an act can last a lifetime. If this book stops one person from committing the act of suicide, then it was worth putting myself out there just for that one individual.

Another reason I wrote this book is to help clinicians who are working to not give up on us, but to assist us to maintain stability. We are human beings who can be very complicated indeed, so be generous with the encouraging word. There were times where I just "hung on to" encouraging words from therapists, psychiatrists and others in the mental health field. You have a very important job!

This book is based solely on my own memories and through journals I have kept over the years. I stuck to the truth and do not expect everyone to understand or agree with the contents in this book. Many names have been changed to protect the privacy of people.

The most important reason I wrote this book is to glorify God for what He has done in my life. He pulled me out of the miry clay and gave me a purpose in life, which is to serve Him. While serving Him, I serve others! Without Him, I would have never been able to write this book. Without Him, I would never have survived living with this illness. I am not ashamed of having Bipolar Disorder. I am just very grateful to still be alive to tell my story.

Chapter 1

Childhood

Even as a small child I guess you could have called me a little entertainer. My mother tells me that I would look for and receive a lot of attention beginning at a very young age. Being the littlest blonde girl of four daughters, people would often tell me that I was cute. It seemed that adults would gravitate toward me, I suppose, because I was the youngest, and the youngest does seem to get the most attention in a family. I can just barely remember being at the local grocery store as a three year old and smiling at the manager of the store as he would ruffle my hair and hand me a lollypop. I would also go up to complete strangers, tug on their pant leg and say "I love you!" with a big smile on my face. Their eyes would light up and I would feel so warm and loved inside even as my mother would apologize and pull me away from them.

My mother has told me the story many times of me as a three year old pulling open the front zipper of a tent we were using for camping. My mother and her friend Lois always got up early and made the coffee and talked. She said that she and Lois would love to see the little blonde curly top in the pink zipper suit opening up the tent with a wide grin on my face. I don't remember that, but I am sure I knew I was loved very much. To this day, if I wear pink, my mother calls me "Little Nance."

I found out much later in life that I was born with one of my hips out of its socket. The doctor who put my hip back into its place had me wear a brace on my leg to hold it and let it grow naturally. He told my parents that it would never bother me in the future and surprisingly it never did.

My oldest sister, Chris, was five when I was born. Gini was four and Linda, who, in all actuality really was the cutest, was two and a half. Growing up with my sisters was great. It was as though we always had constant playmates and every toy in the house was for girls. Linda and I shared a bedroom and would play for hours on end. Maybe we would play "house" and she was the mother and I was the baby, or "school" where we would line up our baby dolls in a row and teach them how to read and write, even if we barely knew how ourselves. Gini and Chris would join us sometimes and we would make forts in the dining room and play cat and mouse games. It seemed as though my young life was filled with a lot of fun and my family babied me whether they meant to or not.

When all three of my sisters were in school, instead of being lonely, I would relish the time that I had my mother all to myself. She would allow me to play our Barbara Streisand and Peter, Paul and Mary records. I loved to sing and my mother encouraged me by clapping for me after each song I sang. I used to sing along with a Barbara Streisand song that went something like "I'm five, I'm five, I'm a big girl now I'm five..." and at the end Ms. Streisand would recite her birthday which was one day shy of my mother's. Because of that song I still to this day get my mother's birthday mixed up with Barbara Streisand's.

Music played a big part in my childhood and I would pretend to be singing in front of large audiences. I suppose most children brought up in the era of the 60's have had similar upbringings. We were sheltered from the storm of the Vietnam War and were just happy little girls growing up with the Walton's, Adam 12, and The Brady Bunch on television.

Kindergarten was a joy to me and the best part was coming home half the day to spend time with my mother. Each day she would ask me what I wanted for lunch. "Would you like a peanut butter and jelly sandwich or a bowl of chicken noodle soup?" I loved that she would let me make the choice and we would sit at the table and eat together whichever I had chosen. I felt very close to my mother and I knew that she loved me very, very much.

The bedroom that Linda and I shared was medium sized with lots of windows dressed with curtains with Noah's Ark characters on them. My father had built a pink dresser with big drawers for Linda and me to share and he also built our beds. Linda's was a regular bed down below, but mine was a bit...eccentric. It hung in midair by four brightly painted yellow chains. It was so high that my father built a little ladder for me to climb up. The chains were secured in the attic, and I never worried that my bed would fall down or that a chain would break loose. I really liked when Linda would move her bed so that it wasn't directly under mine but sideways so that I could see her beautiful face when we chatted at night before we went to sleep. It was always "Nance, you awake?" or "Lin, you awake?"

Because we had a lot of land surrounding us, we also always had fun playing outside. I believe we had the most unique outdoor "toys" in the neighborhood, and anyone who grew up around us remembers them to this day. My parents got a new washer and dryer so my father took apart the old ones and we actually would spin on the inside of the washer in the back yard. There was a nice sized hill in the front yard and one of us, or the neighborhood kids, would curl up inside the inside of the dryer and we would push them as hard as we could and they would stay in the spin cycle all the way down the hill. When they got to the bottom, we would help them out. Personally, I preferred playing in the washer; in fact, I used to have the washer right next to a bush so I would grab on to this bush and make myself twirl. Again, I was picturing myself in front of large audiences and making up songs. One day I was twirling and singing and the words were "All the little children..." when suddenly I heard someone snickering. It was a girl who lived in one of the houses behind us. I quickly stopped singing as I was quite embarrassed. But then I decided to start up again. I didn't care if she made fun of me! We called the inside of the washer "the Roundy-Round."

The other outdoor "toy" was a large barrel that we had rescued from the local lake. We used to walk on the barrel and see how far we could go. That was kind of the evidence, besides our Dad building our dressers and beds, that our father was very frugal and had an imagination for us to play with these household items. Some kids may have only had a trampoline in the back yard to jump on.

I am writing this about my childhood so that it is completely understood by the reader that I had never experienced any abuse or mistreatment of any kind growing up. I enjoyed elementary school very much, and in 2nd and 3rd grade I would write stories that were put into book form with crayon drawings for each one. Both my teachers during those years encouraged me to write more and more stories, and my 3rd grade teacher, Mrs. Anderson, used to tell me that I would become a writer when I grew up. My mother and her friends also encouraged me to write.

I did well in school, but when I reached the 5th grade I discovered that we students were suddenly split up into four groups. There was the "A" group for the smartest kids; the "B" group for the next smartest kids; the "C" group for the average ones, and then the lowest group; the "D" group which, sadly enough, we called the "D is for Dummies" group. Well, I was in the "B" group and very happy to be there because I was known as the smartest girl in that class. I used to let other students cheat off me during tests and it felt good to be called "the smart one." This all ended when some of my teachers had a conference with my mother and suggested I would be better off in the "A" group because when starting high school I would have the most challenging classes if I kept my grades up. I was very disappointed to be moved in the middle of the year into the "A" group where I was no longer known as the smart one, but now I felt like the dumbest one in the class. I was amazed at the difference in the two groups and just how smart these children were.

To me, being moved into this new classroom setting was almost like changing schools. But then a new girl named Carol Scott came to our school. Carol was a tall girl with thick reddish brown hair and I was so happy to no longer be the new girl that I automatically became friends with her. That, in turn, began a friendship that lasted a lifetime. We both had the middle name of "Jean" and so we added our friend Toni whose middle name was also "Jean" and another new girl named "Jane". We would run around arm in arm during recess repeating "Three Jeans and a Jane!"

The summer I was going into 6th grade, our family took a trip across the country for a little over a month. I believe back then many families travelled that way, and we met so many OTHERS at the campgrounds where we stayed. My parents mapped out the trip and we travelled in a yellow Volkswagen bus. Because she had her permit, my sister, Chris was allowed to drive. However, when she was driving, my other two sisters and I would snicker and make fun, so my parents put an abrupt end to that by telling us we were not to say a single word while Chris was driving. Each time we got close to another state line, Chris then took the wheel so that she could say that she drove into each state.

The trip was long and sometimes boring to me at the time. I missed my friends, especially Carol Scott. We kept a log of everyday events in a notebook and I wrote letters to my friends and mailed them, telling them how much I missed them. Remember, at that time there were no computers or cell phones. We saw Mt. Rushmore, The Redwood Forest, The Grand Canyon, Yellowstone National Park, Yosemite National Park, The Golden Gate Bridge and the list went on and on. When we went to the Grand Canyon, we saw cameramen filming a man standing on the edge of the canyon smoking a cigarette. He was wearing a cowboy hat and had a shirt tossed over his shoulder as if he were posing. There was a big beautifully groomed golden dog sitting next to him. They were filming a Marlboro cigarette commercial, and this guy was "the Marlboro Man." Times have truly changed!

My father was always watching how much we spent on everything, and it is still all recorded in the notebooks—how much money each camp ground cost and any museum or place of amusement.

We encountered many storms during that trip.

Driving through Kansas and Oklahoma we ran into some major storms. Looking out of the window far to the east I saw two tornadoes with my own two eyes. I kept yelling "A tornado! Oh, my god, another one! Look!" But my sisters would not look and my mother kept saying "Don't worry, Nancy, it is just a lot of rain coming down in one spot," but I knew better. The radio, before it turned into nothing but crackling, had sounded an emergency alarm.

We were in Gary, Indiana, and had just set up the tent when a storm started brewing. Looking straight up into the sky a person could see the clouds swirling around in a circle, like a funnel. Some elderly people in a small camper asked if we would like to go into their camper for shelter, so Linda and I did. My mother stated later that she wasn't sure if she made the right decision by letting us go into a camper with strangers. Looking back, I say," what was the point of that?" If a tornado had actually come to full fruition, that camper would have been sent across the state.

The very worst storm we endured was actually during another vacation where our tent was set up at Virginia Beach when Hurricane Agnes hit in the middle of the night. The wind and rain were so strong that had we known it was a hurricane we probably would have freaked out. As it was, we all had to pile into the Volkswagen bus and drive to a "safe place," which meant we were parked next to a building as our shelter. We spent the next day at the Laundromat, since everything was wet, including our sleeping bags. One thing I remember about that night was that prior to going to sleep everyone was saying "Good Night," except me. I was mad at one of my sisters, and so I said "Bad night!" Did I have a premonition, or was it a coincidence?

Thus, my fascination for storms began. When we got home, I took out every book I could find about tornadoes from the library. I learned that the meteorologists believed that there was lightning inside the funnel as it plowed through the land. Also, a story I thought was so interesting was about a home that was completely destroyed, but they found a phonograph machine in the rubble and the record still on it was entitled "Stormy Weather."

So, with that said, I am told that I have been in every state in the union in a "camp" environment except Alaska and Hawaii.

I really loved school and did well as far as grades were concerned. When I reached 9th grade, I received straight A's my first semester and I was so happy, but my mother said, "Well, you can only go one way with your grades now, and that would be down." I never understood why she said that. I guess she didn't want to pressure me to get straight A's. My sisters all did well, so the teachers just figured I would too. I joined the track team and enjoyed doing the long jump. I also had been in the band since 5th grade playing the trumpet. I had a lot of encouragement from my family as well as others to excel with the trumpet, which I did.

Life went on without any drama as I began to babysit often for extra money. I loved going to the mall with my friends and even signed up for Charm School with a friend through Montgomery Ward's Department Store. The school was called "Wendy Ward's Charm School" and met once a week. As it turned out, my friend who signed me up for this was busy playing softball, so my mother usually dropped me off by myself. It was there in charm school I learned how to wear make-up and keep my hair (in) "styled" —not just cut. For some reason I was unable to get to the "school" at the time for the younger girls, so I had the opportunity to meet in the group for the older teenager girls. They all seemed so mature and beautiful. We were also introduced to dieting and fashion. I remember the young girl who, I believe, was Wendy Ward herself, the daughter of the owner of Montgomery Wards. At the end of the course we got to pick out outfits from the store and had a fashion show. I believe that the girls in charge helped us choose an outfit that looked just right on us. I was so excited about the outfit that I chose because it fit me perfectly and I got to keep it. It was an indigo blue jumpsuit that zipped up the front and had a decorative hood, along with a scarf to match. They taught us to walk a runway and turn around and walk back. I absolutely loved it! However, I remember going on a diet with my sisters and I went from 123 pounds to 110. Because I got so thin and didn't eat correctly, I started skipping my period. My oldest sister, Chris, was home from college that summer and she lost a lot of weight too. My mother took me to the doctor concerning the loss of my period and when the doctor saw the weight loss on the scale, he put two and two together. The doctor told me that if I didn't gain some weight I would have to give me something called a "pap smear" which would include certain strange things that I wanted nothing to do with! That was when I began eating again. I didn't care if I got fat; I just wanted my period to start up without having anything invasive done at the doctor's office! It finally did and I didn't have to go back to the doctor. What a relief!

There was another experience with the store concerning the charm school. My girlfriend Toni and I had been dropped off at the store one Saturday. It happened to be the day before Easter. We had started doing something that was risky, scary, and gave us a thrill! We were experimenting with shoplifting. Both of us snuck around the nail polish aisle and each stole a bottle of nail polish and put it in our purses. There had been a man there who actually watched me take it and I remember looking at him with defiance as if to say "Go ahead, make my day." Well, he certainly did! As Toni and I strolled down the mall that same man came up to us from behind and grabbed the both of us by the shirt collar. "Is there something in your purse that doesn't belong there, Miss?" He stared me down, eye to eye. Suddenly, I felt a wave of nausea pulse through my stomach along with intense fear. He took us into a back office, and since we both were under-aged (14 or 15 years old), he said he was going to call our parents. I was mortified because I knew that all of my sisters were home because of the Easter holiday. My father and mother piled all of my sisters into the car and brought them down to where I was...sitting in a room with my friend, bawling my eyes out and knowing that I was in big trouble. My father made me apologize to this man, as if I hadn't already, and then made me walk through Sears with all of them looking at tractors. I was so awfully embarrassed! When we finally did get home, my father told everyone to go to their rooms. Sitting in the living room, still crying, I listened to my father's words "Have you ever seen your mother or me steal anything? It is not something a McCurdy would do!" Then, the worst punishment he could have ever given me came to pass. He made me go in my room and get all of my nail polish and remover and clippers. I had to take off my nail polish and trim my nails real short (I always prided myself on my long fingernails). He told me to throw away all of my nail polish, remover, nail files, and even any perfume I may have had. I was finally released and went to bed. The next morning, Easter, I was scheduled to play my trumpet at The Prince of Peace Lutheran church with some other instrumentalists from high school. All I could think of was that people were looking at my short plain nails as I moved the keys on my trumpet.

The summer before 11th grade I used to babysit every weekday for the three children of a well-to-do family in Cortland. I got to their house at 7:00 AM and left at 3:00 PM in the afternoon. They paid me $80.00 a week, which I thought was a lot of money. I got very close to these kids and had a great time with them throughout the summer. The parents worked two different shifts and it seemed kind of strange to me that they only spent a few hours together during the night, and that was it except on weekends. Actually, I was with their children much longer than either one of them. They later called me "the best babysitter anyone could have," probably because I made everything fun for the children. The only thing I didn't like was having no time to sleep in during the week. That was something that I didn't think of when I committed to take that summer job.

During those high school years my personality was very strong. I loved to joke around a lot and have all my friends laughing. I was invited to many sleepovers where I would stay up all night entertaining my girlfriends, eating junk food and laughing a lot. Even though I would get on some of their nerves, they always knew that I would make them laugh in the end. We made prank phone calls, watched scary movies, danced, and had great times together. My best friend was Candice Maples. (She was the one who got me signed up for charm school.) I spent many nights at her house and we always had a great time. She also had a tremendous sense of humor and we loved to giggle together on into the night.

I actually had a few best friends and my friend Frankie and I used to play sports in the summer at each other's homes along with practicing our trumpets together. I used to look forward to band camp as much as Christmas. I was a real ham with my trumpet, but I also had a competitive spirit and had to be the best. Once I turned 16, I got my silver flare trumpet and began playing solos on an ongoing basis. I just dearly loved band and my three sisters were also a part of band. Chris played the sax and the baritone sax along with the tuba in marching band, Linda played the sax and the trombone, and Gini was a master of the clarinet and played the baritone in the marching band. I stuck with the trumpet for concert and marching band and loved being known as the "star" trumpet player for our school.

As far as church was concerned, all I remember was being dropped off a few times at the local Methodist church with my sisters and then picked up afterward. I hated every minute of it because I didn't understand it and I was extremely embarrassed when I asked a group of girls, "Whose picture was that up in the church?" It was of a man with long brown hair. I thought he didn't fit in with the old white haired man who was leading the boring service. They laughed at me. "That's Jesus!" In my young mind I thought, "Well, who IS HE?" But I kept my mouth shut not to be embarrassed even worse. Apparently, everyone knew who he was but me. My parents didn't talk about Jesus. My mother did say prayers with us sometimes at night, but they were just "God Bless Mother, God Bless Daddy, God Bless…" So I thought praying meant that you "God Bless everyone you know in your family." In fact, when I got a little older and insisted on going to a Baptist Vacation Bible School at a church down the road from our home, they talked all about Jesus. I was so excited the last day of the Bible school when I came home. As my mother opened the front door I said "Mom! I got saved from Jesus!" My mother burst out laughing. There I was again, being laughed at because of this man named Jesus. I wanted nothing more to do with church, and any and all "religious" desire was gone.

At this time, my father worked at the local steel mill in the engineering department, and my mother had gone back to school and gotten her Master's degree in Education. My mother was hired at Lakeview Middle School as a teacher for the Learning Disabled. My sister Chris graduated from Kent State with a degree in Public Relations, my sister Gini was going to Bowling Green University in Toledo for an RN degree and later got her degree as a nurse anesthetist, and Linda ended up also going to Kent State to pursue a degree in business. It was expected of me to go to college. Now, looking back in my life, I believe I have the highest education of anyone in my family. I have a PhD. from the University of Bipolar.

Chapter 2

The First Depression

The day it began, I can't say. The length of time it took to deepen, I don't remember. All I knew was that, I, Nancy McCurdy, as real as this book is in your hands, was losing the most important part of my being: my mind!

Who would have ever thought that I would get depression? After all, I was a very popular, well-adjusted girl who came from a good middle class loving family. To have an illness of the mind was totally foreign for the McCurdy household as well as Lakeview Local Schools and anywhere else my sad self would go. Where did this strange behavior pattern come from? As I reached my 17th birthday in July of 1979 my life began to unravel. It started creeping up on me as my senior year loomed ahead at the end of August. Every thought that came into my head was negative. Dark. Ugly. When school started, I went, not knowing what to say to my friends. I was afraid that people would find out that my mind was broken. Oh! The humiliation of it all! There I was at the beginning of my senior year in high school; the best year and the most fun I would ever have in school, or possibly the "best time of my life!" —or so I had always heard. But as each day passed, the negativity, insecurity, and emotional pain grew worse and worse. I cried out to my family. "Help me!" My mother called the local mental health center and made an appointment with a counselor there.

This was just the beginning of 30 years of psychiatry which painfully entered my life; in all actuality, it took over every aspect of my being. The counselor was a young man just out of college. He had no idea what was wrong with me or what to do for me. I sat in his office holding on to a glimmer of hope that this man may somehow be of help to take this misery away. I looked into his eyes for answers, but he was just appeasing me with words. He, Mr. Lolume, had no idea how to treat the symptoms of depression. Every week my mother would get off work and drive me to the mental health center in Warren to talk to this man. He asked me in indirect ways questions that concerned my family; for example, was my father molesting me? I did not like him. He didn't explain to me that my depression was caused by a chemical imbalance in the brain because I don't think he knew that. He just kept searching for reasons "why" I was in this black mindset that stayed with me 24/7. Mr. Lolume became disgusting to me and I was becoming more and more aware that he didn't know how to help me in any way, shape, or form. The only relief I had was when I went to sleep, and I had a hard time doing that!

Finally, out of complete despair, I showed my parents just how unhappy I truly was. That day I was in the house with my father when my mother came home from the grocery store and drove her light yellow Pontiac close to the back door of the house. As soon as I saw her park the car, I ran outside screaming at the top of my lungs. I lay down right next to the front wheels of the car and took hold of the grass with both hands with the right side of my body up against the tires. I screamed so loud I may have startled the neighbors. I yelled "Run over me! Smash my brain! Run over me!" as the tears rolled down my face. "Kill me, please, Mom!" I ripped up the grass in both hands driving pieces of dirt under my fingernails. I was so desperate I was literally asking my mother to kill me. My father, in a state of utter shock and confusion said to me, "Is that any way to greet your mother?"

The very next day I had an appointment with a psychiatrist at the same mental health center. She was a lovely Asian woman with a beautiful voice. She gave me a prescription, just one, of Stelazine. I did not know what Stelazine was or what it was supposed to do, but my mother gave this pill to me every morning. The only thing that I noticed was that it made me feel very drowsy and a bit dopey. Now, not only did I walk the halls of the school with negative, depressive thoughts, I walked in a daze from this odd medication. All of my friends, Candice, Dena, Toni, Jane, Frankie and Pamela were dumbfounded at the difference in their friend. A lot of them told me to "just go back to being yourself again!" Oh! If they only knew how badly I wanted to! I could not find the girl I used to be, this one had a new brain and an entirely different personality! This new brain only signaled negativity and fear, forgetting any and all pleasure or happiness. It was like living out a horror movie each and every day...and night!

I was told to see the school counselor, Mrs. Roads. During study hall I sat squirming in my chair as Mrs. Roads tried guessing what was the matter with me. Like the therapist, Mr. Lolume, Mrs. Roads did not know me prior to this problem which meant that she wasn't sure if this truly was new behavior or if this had been an ongoing problem. Unfortunately, Mrs. Roads was not that much help either. I kept spiraling down. One of the hardest parts of going through a deep chemical depression is not being able to function as you always did. As each student makes their mark in high school, one of the most attractive attributes my friends had enjoyed about me was comedy. In fact, I was voted "Most Comical" by my peers. This was a huge problem now because there were simply no jokes to tell and not a single thing that was at all funny to my mind. Most of my friends who had known me since kindergarten, out of ignorance, began to avoid me at school, not knowing what to say, or how to deal with this new behavior which was the opposite of who I had been.

The other most important attribute I was known for was my trumpet playing. In fact, I loved my trumpet so much prior to becoming depressed, I would practice before school, during school and after school! There was never a night that my trumpet didn't come home with me! As I grew up, I had had a lot of encouragement with my trumpet playing. When I was 16, the band director strongly recommended to my parents that they buy me a silver trumpet. When I went with my parents and purchased this new "used" trumpet, I brought it home and immediately began practicing all the songs that were given out at band. I usually had the song memorized before the band had even tried it. So, when the band played "Boogey Woogey Bugle Boy" for the first time, I played it loud and clear with full confidence. And I was the **only** one in the band that knew how to play it!

Well, now that I was depressed, I still had to perform the same as I always had--playing solos and never making a mistake. This was extremely difficult for me to do because with depression comes insecurity. The expectation of being the solo trumpet player became too much to bear. I also had the fear that someone would take on a "challenge," as they called it in band, to see if they could play better than I. My self-esteem and thoughts were so dark that I felt it would happen any day.

Horror in the Trumpet Section

Then it happened. My worst nightmare! We were on the field for a band night and had just gotten into concert formation. There were two songs that we played that year while standing still in this particular position. One was "Love me Tender" by Elvis and the other was "Stayin' Alive" by the Bee Gees. Here we were starting the song "Love Me Tender" which, of course, started out slow and quiet with the trumpet section leading at the beginning of the song, when I started blaring out "Stayin Alive" as loud as I possibly could (yes, loud as usual) until I realized that I was the only one playing the wrong song. I was so embarrassed and all I could think of was dying. Ironically the song was called "Stayin' Alive" but I was thinking: death! *"Please let me just drop dead!"* I thought to myself over and over. Afterward, Mr. Bob Fleming himself, (my trumpet teacher from Youngstown State University & the best trumpet player known to mankind) came up to me and said "McCurdy, when you make a mistake, you make a whopper!" Other students came up to me and laughed about it, but I sat there in the bleachers by myself with a sense of doom and loneliness like I had never felt before. It hurt to even breathe. To try to save myself from any further humiliation, I began skipping school. Although I felt even worse when I did this, I would wait until my parents left the house in the morning, hiding on the far side of the house until the coast was clear. When I watched the cars pull out of the drive-way, I would go into the house and wander around all day. Sleeping was impossible, and now accompanying this deep seated depression a new problem began to arise called anxiety. Pacing and pacing throughout the house in a nervous, fear-driven manner was even more than I could bear. It wasn't long until the word *Suicide* began to seep throughout my thought pattern. Suicide. Death! Finally there was a way out!

The first concrete thought of suicide electrified my thought pattern like a wave of extreme fear. Fear that overwhelmed my soul, but it also brought a spark of hopefulness. Will this be my fate? Lying in bed one night in a fitful sleep I thought about the possibility of committing suicide. There was only one way to do it: to lock myself in the bathroom, fill the sink up with water and put my curling iron in the water to electrocute myself. That was the only way that I could think of. I told my parents of my plan but never went through with it because of how badly they freaked out when I locked the bathroom door.

At a time when most seniors in high school are thinking about "What they wanted to be when they grew up?" I was way ahead of them. What did I want to be...BEFORE I grew up? A tombstone. For many years I obsessively wandered aimlessly around cemeteries and fantasized about death. Since I did not know of an afterlife, I believed I would just have my body decay under the ground with ants, worms, maggots and anything else crawling around my corpse. I would be the beautiful bride of Frankenstein. Of course; prior to the tombstones, I thought about my funeral...I planned my funeral, several times over. All the mourners would look down at my young body displayed with every curl in place, eyes closed with mascara covering my eyelashes until they were lavishly curled upward. My lips would be in a perfect pout with bright red lipstick to match the flowers that some stupid person would send as though they cared about me and my family. Maybe I would leave behind my make-up to my friend Chrissy who loved make-up too. She would have been so sad to see me die. Sometimes I truly believe that I completely understand grief, although I have not had a close loved one die during my life at the time of writing this. I grieved over my own death so many times that I felt that I actually did die! I mourned. Then it would be over until my next fantasy about death. Post mortem. I really would not have minded having my little foot sticking out there in the morgue with a tag on my big toe. The tag would have the word LOSER written in large letters. These were primarily the kinds of thoughts I obsessed over.

In the fall of 1979, my sister Chris was preparing to marry Keith Brown. I remember going into her bedroom one night when she was home getting ready for her wedding, and I woke her up to tell her how depressed I was. Many years later she told me that she remembers how odd it was to her that I was in this horrible 'funk' when she was so excited during the days leading up to her wedding. She couldn't understand, as it seemed *no one* could understand, the horrific emotional pain I was suffering. Even in my despair, I actually played my trumpet for my sister's wedding with a pianist. My Grandmother told me afterwards how beautiful the song was, and that it was the first time she really heard how well I played the trumpet. It was bittersweet for her to say that and also showed that no matter how I felt that day, I would never make a mistake again with my trumpet! Never! No never! I didn't want anyone to know how depressed I really was and I thought messing up a solo again would be definite proof that something really bad was going on with me. That is why I kept practicing even though it was more than just a struggle.

Keeping in mind that nobody understood what was wrong with me, I was constantly asking for help; in fact, I was asking for help for over ten years, telling my story to anyone who would listen. There was always a faint glimmer of hope that somebody, somewhere, somehow would have an answer to the horror I was enduring. It took many years of the ups and downs of manic depression until I finally did find an answer to my emotional pain…a reason NOT to commit suicide.

Since the depression and severe anxiety never let up, the psychiatrist really did not seem to have any answers for me and the Stelazine that she prescribed for me did nothing to relieve the torture in my mind. Going to the therapist was of no help either. In fact, it made things worse because he really had no clue what was wrong and how to deal with it. It just seemed so hopeless. I was struggling through my journalism class knowing that the second half of my senior year would mean speech class. The thought of making a speech terrified me and I determined that the only way to get out of making speeches and making a fool of myself was to commit suicide beforehand. Problems were arising in all of my classes and Mrs. Roads made it her business to speak to each of my teachers to let them know that there was a psychological problem going on. This caused a painful new mindset that stayed with me all day long both at school and at home. It was called paranoia. I believed that not only my friends and all the other students were aware of a problem with my mind but now even the teachers were talking about me behind my back. I felt this "hush" whisper when I walked by certain people in the hallways. It was so difficult to continue going to school, but Mr. Lalome had told me that if I skipped any more days then a truant officer would "make" me go to school. I had never been in trouble at school before and was very afraid of a truant officer, although I didn't really know exactly what the term meant.

It was Halloween 1979. I had been part of the Beta Club for four years and they were holding their annual Halloween party at The Optimist Club (yes, ironic name for me at the time) near my home. I decided to dress up like an old man and talk in my special low voice for the party. It was very difficult to be around all of my friends while feeling depressed and this night was no different from the usual deep emotional pain I was suffering with. I was aware that I was expected to joke around and so I made up my mind to make jokes that evening although nothing seemed funny. Right at the time I was thinking this, a boy in a wheelchair came into the room. My mind was not quick to think things through, and I didn't even recognize that this was a boy from my school who was wheelchair bound from some type of affliction. Loud and clear I announced "Oh look, he dressed like an invalid!" It only took a second for me to realize my mistake. And it was no joke.

Embarrassment and confusion took over and again I wanted to die right then and there. Literally, die. The school was unforgiving. My friends thought I just wanted attention. The rumors began. "What is wrong with Nancy?" "Has she truly lost her mind?" I became increasingly quiet at school. This was so *not* my nature that people really were wondering what happened to this happy-go-lucky girl who always made them laugh. The thoughts were so negative that I could not bear it, but bear it, I did. There was nothing changing and the thoughts of suicide roamed in and out of my mind. I truly thought that I would suffer with this deep dark depression forever.

Chapter 3

The First Mania

It was near December of 1979 when suddenly there was a significant and almost freaky change in my mind and behavior. Instead of the negative, painful thoughts, a spark of excitement took their place. In fact, the excitement took over completely. Without knowing what was going on, I became more and more talkative, more confident and more charming than ever before in my life. My friends and family were just as amazed as they watched this person who was so very down-in-the-dumps and unable to verbalize transform into this outgoing super chick with an answer for everything. How exciting it was for me to be in a speech class! After all this kind of attention was what I was looking for! In January, at the speech banquet, I made a hilarious speech about people's most embarrassing moments and had everyone in an uproar of laughter. I had interviewed my friends and family and found out some really funny embarrassing moments.

The trumpet playing became an obsession and I started playing the Pink Panther theme in a jazz form in front of the entire school for pep rallies in the gym. The band director was so thrilled to have his star trumpet player back, he allowed me to utilize my talent more and more. Maybe it was scary for others to watch the behavior change. In my mind, it was the best thing that ever happened to me! It was very hard for *me* to believe that just months before I was seriously contemplating suicide. I had no idea who *that* girl was as I reveled in this everyday mood that kept on getting higher and higher. I woke up each morning happy, so *very* happy to start the day. I began noticing boys more and started flirting with them, not knowing what to make of it myself.

When I began waitressing at a local ice cream restaurant called Friendly's, a boy who was four years older than me began asking me out on dates. Tom was insistent and I began going out with him and for the first time I really tried drinking alcohol. Tom drank a lot and introduced me to alcohol and marijuana very quickly. I sometimes felt uncomfortable around Tom, but yet he was persistent.

One evening I was invited to a party at the home of one of my friends, and I asked Tom to take me. On the way there, he took out a marijuana cigarette and shared it with me. This was the first time that I actually breathed in the heavy smoke and immediately began to experience a mental change. As we walked into my girlfriend's house, it was apparent that everyone was enjoying themselves. Suddenly, I began hallucinating. There was a woman named Susan there who was laughing and I saw her laughing in slow motion like in a movie. Then there was the pizza. In my mind, the pizza started to turn into spaghetti and began flying around the room. The host of the party, Tina, saw what was happening and decided to put me upstairs into her bed. As I lay on this pink ruffled bed in Tina's beautiful bedroom, my mind and heart started racing until I felt that I was ready to burst. That really scared Tom who now decided that I needed some medical attention and practically carried me to the car and drove me home. My parents were informed of what had happened, and my father, seeing his daughter talking completely out of her mind, knew that she needed help. I sat in the back seat as both my parents drove me to the emergency room with Tom following close behind. I told my Dad to hurry up because my heart was beating so hard and loud that I myself was scared, even though I was out of touch with reality. When we reached the hospital, I was taken right into a room and told to lie down on the bed. Just then a young doctor walked in to talk to me and I hallucinated that this doctor was Sylvester Stallone. As I kept repeating that I was so excited to meet this very famous star of the newly released movie Rocky, all of the nurses were laughing. They knew the doctor and knew that he was definitely not this film star that I seriously believed that he was. And I was not just asking for his autograph, but asking him to join me on the bed. My parents were then called into the room and I heard the doctor say, "Your daughter is just extremely high. There is nothing that we can do for her except wait until this drug wears off. The best thing to do is to take her home and let her sleep until the marijuana leaves her system."

This was probably the first major sign that there was truly something seriously wrong with my brain chemicals. The good that came out of it was that it scared me so badly that I vowed to stay away from drugs altogether. After all, my mind could go places where no others have gone *without* using any type of drug.

Another incident occurred when I was invited to drive to Cleveland with a group of friends from high school to see a concert put on by Todd Rundgren. I was so excited to be invited and, mind you, even though depression had disappeared, I was still taking the Stelazine. I had become very close with an exchange student from Sweden who was two years older and much more experienced in life than I was. She actually helped me through the depression I had had for all those months. Well, now, here we are in this van and I was thinking how much fun it was going to be when all the sudden one of the guys took out a bottle of 151 Rum and a shot glass. He asked if anyone wanted to try to drink more than him. Not knowing how strong the booze was and being filled with mischief (and complete naivety) I yelled, "I will!" The first shot went down my throat like a ball of fire. It also hit my nervous system right away and I became delirious. The kid just kept giving me shot after shot and by the time we got to the concert, they had to carry me to my seat. The only thing I remember was throwing up all over the steps that were right next to my seat on the end. People were walking down and I would hear them yell "Eww, gross, someone puked!" I tried to apologize but I had no voice. During the concert I must have been taken to the bathroom several times, barely aware of how many times I got sick. Sitting back in my seat I felt my heartbeat slowing down, down, down and thinking that this was it, I was truly going to die. I thought about how much I had wanted to die months prior to this night, but now, I really *didn't* want to die since I was feeling so much better. How ironic that when I finally decided to live, I was about to die. I did not hear or see any of the concert that night. I did not remember any of it. The next thing I *do* remember was waking up in the morning feeling so very, very sick, and my mind was a big blur. My friend from Sweden had spent the night and we had to go to school that day, the day after New Year's. I told my mother that I was just too sick to make it to school, but she said that if I was sick it was my own fault since I still reeked with the smell of alcohol. She gave me the pill as usual, and my friend and I went off to school. For three terrifying days I went from high mood to low mood to confused mood to angry mood to happy mood to elated mood to suicidal mood. It was horrible. I also could barely eat those three days as I may have had alcohol poisoning along with the prescription drug I was taking. Did I learn a lesson? Yes. Did I continue to get drunk? Yes.

After graduating from high school, I made a bad choice that summer before college that affected my life for the next 12 years. I started smoking cigarettes when I turned 18 years old. That was something that my parents had quit years and years before and it upset both of them to see their daughter begin smoking after all those years of them being against it.

That summer I was somewhat in another realm mentally and was not working. However, I found myself in the Cortland Street Fair Queen Contest at the annual fair. We always used to joke about this contest where local girls were sponsored by local businesses or organizations, calling it the "Street Treat." My sponsor was the Lakeview Band Boosters. I was encouraged by my family and friends to be in the contest, and so I went out and bought two new dresses for the occasion. Four years prior, my sister, Gini, had won "Miss

Congeniality" at the same contest. I really didn't care if I won or not; I actually didn't care to be in it at all at the time!

Prior to the contest, we were given all the questions that the MC would be asking us that night, although we had no idea which one would be *our* question. I did not take this seriously at all and halfheartedly practiced my answers. When the time came that I was called up to the microphone, the MC asked me, "If you had a friend in the hospital, what would you do?" Oh no! I had not figured out an answer to that one! While practicing I had glibly answered that one with "I would give her some medicine." That seemed like a really stupid answer now, in front of all my peers, friends, and well, the entire town! I stood there unable to speak for an uncomfortable amount of time…it probably was seconds but felt like hours. I finally responded with something that I to this day don't remember at all! It was then that I decided I would ALWAYS be prepared to speak in front of people – no matter what my mood was! Although I obviously did not win any prize that night, I certainly learned a lesson and I had a wonderful time riding on the back of my father's yellow Spitfire in the street fair parade throwing out candy to all the children.

That fall I packed up my belongings and moved to Kent State University. My major of choice was "Child Psychology!" How profound! I found myself so enchanted by the parties, the bars, the alcohol, and the boys—you would wonder how I ever learned anything in college. I thought of my French class as a great opportunity to show off my skills with a language that I dearly loved. The class was taught by a beautiful woman we called Mademoiselle Evans. The best teacher I had ever encountered. Her expectations of her students were very high and I, in turn, took French on by storm. The other course that I excelled in was, not surprising, the Kent State marching band. I was second chair trumpet and the only girl trumpet player. I was sure that all the boys who played the trumpet were jealous of me for getting second chair when I was only a freshman. I actually was driving them all crazy with my insistent mouth and over the top self-assurance. After the marching band was over, I joined a band called the Flasherbrass which was a band established to perform just at the basketball games. I drove with a friend to Kent State to play at these basketball games during the December break. However, I was always really late getting there so guys in the trumpet section really got angry with me. The mania caused me to drive erratically through the streets to get to the Kent State gymnasium and my friend would yell at me and hide his head as I swerved from street to street. The guys in the band told me that the director was going to kick me out of the Flasherbrass ensemble for being late all the time. I thought that over, but figured he would never do that since I was the best trumpet player he had next to Roberto who was 1st chair.

This mania, fueled by a lack of any type of medicine (I was off the Stelazine) made this chick I call myself just roar through the halls of the dorm. There was not one girl who lived in Prentice Hall who didn't know who Nancy McCurdy was, and many who did not like me. However, I had no concerns about what other people thought of me during that manic episode.

Then there was the evening that my roommate, Laura Taylor, and I had planned a party in our dorm room. Laura had a wonderful sense of humor and there was a lot of laughter and craziness that went on between us. Laura had only invited her sister, Lonnie and her boyfriend, Ryan to the party. When I began getting call after call to escort the people coming to my party, an awkward major problem quickly arose. Each and every person whom I had invited had been male. Worse than that, most of them expected to be my "date" for the night. As the small dorm room began to fill up, I began to panic. Laura was downstairs working at the sandwich shop so the only other girl was Lonnie, Laura's sister. I ran downstairs several times to ask Laura to hurry and close up shop because she was needed. It was not only embarrassing but humiliating. Although, my mood was so high it didn't seem quite so bad at the time. How exciting that all these boys wanted to come to my party! If none of the girls in the dorm wanted to join in on my amazing party it was they who missed out. After all, there were so many boys that attended; seriously, the entire floor could have had a great time! What was their problem?

When the mania finally made its disconcerting switch to depression, I was mortified looking back on that night.

There was one girl (and I'm sure others) who absolutely hated me playing my trumpet. I knew that Kate didn't like hearing my trumpet so I would go downstairs with Laura, call Kate on the phone and blast my trumpet into the phone as loud and obnoxious as I could be. Laura and I would laugh and laugh. I also would get in trouble for playing my stereo so loud that it literally shook the room.

As I mentioned, I just loved my French classes and Mme. Evans. I would go in front of the class and sing songs like "The Answer is Blowing in the Wind" in French. It was beautiful to me. Learning how to read and write French was really something I was interested in and it was such a romantic language. Mme. Evans seemed to like me and probably just thought that I was a high strung girl. The interesting thing was that nobody was with me 24 hours a day so nobody could see that I was a powerhouse every single hour of every single day. I was also not sleeping. Christmas break would prove to be the "peak" of mania which was quite devastating and downright scary for my family.

First off, I insisted on being in this beauty/talent pageant that was held in Niles, close to home but quite a way from Kent State University. One of my boyfriends paid the $50.00 for me to participate in this contest. I wore an old prom dress that belonged to one of my sisters and brought my trumpet along. When it came to the talent part of it I played "The Godfather" on my trumpet and dazzled the judges with my magnetic charm that mania always brings. I ended up winning 1st runner-up which included an enormous green trophy which was shiny and very tall and it had a big gold star on it. I was so proud of myself I was screaming to everyone in the dorm, "I won 1st runner-up in a beauty pageant! I won 1st runner-up in a beauty pageant!" There was a girl walking down the hall and she looked over at me in this flowing green prom dress and screamed at the top of her lungs, "SO WHAT!" This didn't stop me in any way; in fact, I thought it was hilarious that the girl had such a reaction.

I was always the center of attention and if I wasn't, I would make myself be somehow. I once planned to dye my hair purple so that I could be in People magazine. Little did I know at the time that it would be a trend of the future to dye your hair off-the-wall colors.

Delusion of Grandeur: Who do I believe?

This strange "power" of believing that I could do anything came to an abrupt culmination while I was home on Christmas break. My sister and I were watching a movie late one night; probably around 11:30 PM. She had some marijuana and asked me to join her in smoking it. I felt like I was safe this time, home with my sister, what could go wrong if she was smoking it with me? I inhaled just a few puffs when suddenly I began hallucinating. As I looked at the television, I could tell what they were thinking when they were making the movie, such as, "Gee, I wonder if I said that line correctly." Or, "Isn't the make-up man going to take care of my hair before this next head shot?" I asked my sister what she was feeling. She stated that she just felt a regular high like any other time that she smoked pot. I started to panic because my heart was racing and I was just plain feeling weird. My sister was absolutely furious when I felt compelled to wake up our parents to let them know that we had smoked pot and that I was feeling strange. Soon our father got up and got a drink of water from the kitchen, passing the two of us in the living room. I was feeling better by this time and my sister said that the only reason he went to get a glass of water was to check-up on us. When it became really late, near four in the morning, I was sure the pot had worn off since my sister told me it had worn off hours ago. We finally decided to go to bed in our separate bedrooms since my other two sisters had moved out. Everything seemed fine, and I was very tired. Little did I know that I was about to experience something that would influence my life drastically.

I opened the door to my bedroom, walked in and shut the door behind me. Looking around, I was amazed and terrified at the same time. My bedroom was all lit up, filled with a bright light that illuminated every inch of space; it was, to say the least, amazing to me. Everything sparkled. There was one message being sent to my brain and one message only. "Nancy, you will become famous," was the message. It was just this supernatural knowledge that I was going to become famous. Soon, there were some more major signs. The extra-large green trophy that I had won in that beauty pageant began to move. It was dancing up and down and the gold star on it shined out as if to say "Look at me! I am proof!" The next clue concerning fame came from a magazine. I was suddenly extremely impressed to read an article in my Cosmopolitan Magazine. It was the life story of Luciana Pavarotti, the famous opera singer. I sat down and took the time to read the entire article which was about how he had been very poor growing up. His life took a turn when he began singing at a young age, and in time became a very well-known and highly paid singer who sang throughout the world. This was also proof.

There were a couple of other things that happened that early morning that just proved to me that I would become famous. I decided to go to bed but lay there shivering in fear with my heart pounding out of my chest. Without understanding prayer, I decided to pray to God because I had to know whether this was true or was I completely losing my mind. I begged God to show me. Suddenly a "spirit" in a large pure white hooded robe stood next to my bed facing me. This "person" was so bright; it was hard to look at him as just his presence lit up my bedroom again. Then, he spoke and said "Yes, Nancy, you will become famous and I will be with you every step of the way." I closed my eyes and opened them only to find that this "person" had disappeared. Then the room went dark since I hadn't even turned the light on. It was the most profound experience that I had ever encountered in my young life and it was extremely exciting to know that an angel, or God, or *someone* had visited me with this interesting news. What was ironic was that years before I used to listen to music and twirl around the living room with my eyes shut and fantasized that I would be singing in front of thousands and thousands of people with whatever song was on the phonograph playing. It had started with Barbara Streisand when I was only five or six years old. Then in high school it would be Chuck

Mangione on the flugelhorn. It could even be a man singing and I would picture myself singing in front of the world. From the beginning of my life, I had fantasized of doing talent in front of thousands. When this experience happened to me at 18 years old, it just seemed to be a confirmation of the life I would lead in my future. Unfortunately, psychiatry and "messages" from God have a long history of mixing together during a manic episode. Over many years, some psychiatrists have told me it could be true while others thought it was a delusion. Who was I to believe? This particular night would come back to the forefront of my mind and heart many times over the course of my life and I can still hear the words spoken by the person wearing the white hooded robe as though it was yesterday.

I was driven by my parents back to Kent State after the Christmas break. They were <u>very</u> concerned with my behavior. When I arrived back at my dorm and was talking with my roommate Laura, she was telling me that she had worked as a bank teller during the Christmas break and that she received a raise and would be offered the job during the summer months. This just seemed so realistic to me compared to what I was sharing about the Christmas break – a promise of fame and fortune from God- now just seemed pretty ludicrous. Could it have been nothing but a delusion? If so, what could be done about it? Things started getting really confusing for me but I have always held on to those 17 words that were spoken so very clearly to me that evening.

Chapter 4

NO, NOT AGAIN!

As the days turned into weeks then into months, January, February, March, it seemed as though I was slowing down. My thought processes were changing again and this time I knew what was slowly creeping up on me. Depression again! The worst nightmare anyone could ever live with was returning. It started to become painful to do anything. Each and every morning I would wake up in fear and despair at exactly 6:00 AM. It was so horrible and I didn't know what to do. I was starting to think about suicide day in and day out. Going to classes seemed close to impossible. Reading a book to study for a test was not an option. Understandably, my French professor noticed right away what was happening to me and she was very concerned.

I starting calling my parents in the mornings telling my mother how depressed I was and that suicide was on my mind. It was hard to know what I was putting my mother through each morning as I called so often when my mother was trying to get dressed and ready for her job at Lakeview Schools as a Special Education teacher. I had taken psychology and had the book I had used for the class. Glancing through the book, the Abnormal Psychology Section caught my eye. Manic Depression: A mental illness that causes extreme high moods and extreme low moods in a pattern.

Depression and mania could each last several months until the chemicals in the brain would change and the mind was once again changed.

It was explained so nicely on paper, but to live it was another story. I wandered around the campus unable to even wear make-up to hide my despair. I wore the same bib overalls every day and night because I was too depressed to change my clothes. I could barely brush my hair, let alone wash it. No longer did I have a skip in my step. No longer did my eyes sparkle with glee and my smile beam for all human kind. I lowered my head in anguish. I was so relieved when people I had known did not recognize me. Then there were those that did. I would see boys whom I had known and they stared at me and would ask "Nancy, is that you?" "No." I would answer sternly. How could I explain myself? It was just like in high school when I couldn't function. I didn't care about anything and could not even fathom that I was the same girl who had had so many boyfriends. All I wanted now was to be left alone. There was no paranoia because I didn't care enough to be worried about other people's thoughts. One day I received a check for over $100.00 from working in the Prentice Hall Cafeteria. I was a different person when I worked there; so vibrant and alive but now I hardly remembered that I had had a job. I had been in charge of desserts. When I was filled with all that manic charm I would tell people I WAS a dessert! Delicious and Delightful! Now I felt Doomed and Damned. I tried to go to classes but I never made it, the emotional pain drained the life out of me. The only class I made it to was French.

Mme. Evans, my French professor watched helplessly as I sat looking at a blank test unable to answer a single question. This was quite frightening to her because she remembered this wild girl who always did very well on tests and was eager to hand them in. She followed me after class that day and I told her how suicidal I was. We were in an elevator leaving class when I, in fear of going back to my dorm, asked her if I could go home with her. She took just a few minutes to think about it and then said "yes." She too was concerned that I would commit suicide. I rode home with her to

Green, Ohio where Mme. Evans lived with her husband and two small children. She told me that she would put me to work doing the dishes after dinner. Her husband seemed less than overjoyed to have this strange suicidal girl staying for dinner and overnight. Mme. Evans showed me my bedroom and I curled up on the bed sweating and fearfully rolling from the left to right in agony. I could overhear her upstairs crying, and I felt like whatever the problem was it must be my fault. In the morning her husband left for work, the children left for school and she and I went to the local high school where she was teaching Elementary French to a high school class. I was introduced as a guest and sat in the front near her.

As the day wore on, I was having trouble sitting in my seat filled with this anguish and emotional torture, so I interrupted the class and told Mme. Evans that I was going for a walk. She wasn't in a position to argue with me. I left the high school and began a journey in that small country town. It started to drizzle, and then it began to pour buckets. I felt immune from the rain as I walked and walked with my blue jean overalls getting drenched. All at once I saw it. A church. A big church with two oversized front doors. I reached the front doors of the church and began pounding on them as if to ask God to let me in. Wasn't anyone there? Couldn't anyone hear me? I started screaming "Answer me! Where are you God? You liar! You horrible liar! Answer this door!" But nobody answered the church doors and I just stood trembling in the rain thinking that even God did not care to help. The emotional pain was unbearable. God had cheated me out of his promised fame. I have only death to look forward to now. The hurt inside my heart ached to the point of near death. Oh, how badly I wanted to die! I curled up into a fetal position and just soaked in the rain and the pain. This was the end. It had to be the end.

Suddenly I remembered where I was and I realized that I had been gone far too long. I walked back to the school and into Mme. Evans' classroom. The look of relief on her face was evident as she was worried that she had lost me. It didn't matter that I was drenched; I could tell she was very relieved that I had come back.

The kids in her class looked at me inquisitively. Mme. Evans was just glad that I was alive.

The phone rang at my parents' home and this time it was Mme. Evans calling them. She had my psychology book in front of her and told my mother, "If you don't come and get your daughter, you will not have a daughter soon." She explained the dire need I was in with suicide filling my head like a wild impulse I could not control. It was then that my parents acknowledged it was time to get me home and get me into some kind of mental health treatment. Nothing was helping at Kent State, although I had called the Health Center and told them I was suicidal and that staying there only made things worse. When I went there the nurses there only said "We were expecting some very overweight, not so good looking girl to walk in here. You don't have a reason to be depressed!"

I cringed as for the first time I realized that there was a stigma attached to people who were suicidal. For years and years afterwards I would hear, "You don't *look* depressed!" I would hear this from everyone; it didn't matter who or where these people were from. Psychiatrists themselves have told me the same thing: "You don't *look* depressed." It was because I quickly learned that I didn't *want* to look depressed. No matter how bad I felt, I attempted to put my make-up on and curl my hair. It was a trick that would serve as a blessing and/or a curse. I learned very quickly that there really was a "look" for people who are in depression. That is when I decided to smile all the time. People had a hard time knowing what was behind the smile. Smiling was a nice cover-up. I say "nice," because people smiled back. But sometimes when I forced a smile, the person did not smile back and I felt like I wasted my already dwindling energy on a smile. Many people would ask me over the years, "What is behind that smile?" Or, if I was at work, the boss would say, "You have a nice smile, but can you do the work?" If I was depressed it would make me cringe inside; if manic, I would smile even bigger knowing that I could conquer any task proposed to me.

When my mother came to Kent State to pick up her depressed daughter and move her back home in the middle of the semester, it made a huge impact on the girls at the dorm. They were also witnesses to this horrific change in their friend, and even the ones who hated me for my loud boisterous bragging and blaring of the trumpet looked at me with concern. "What in the world happened to Nancy, you know—the crazy loud mouth? She is walking around like a lost sheep!" Two Christian girls were praying for me when my mother walked into the room. "Pack everything up, Nancy; you are coming home with me." The two Christian girls looked at my mother and said "No, she is okay now; Nancy is healed from her depression as we just prayed for her." I was in a fog not knowing whether this prayer would work, or if it was time to move home. My mother won and everything that belonged to me was taken from the dorm. Laura, my roommate was the most affected by my actions and cried a lot. She kept asking, "Why are you doing this to me, Nancy?" I had no answers for my own behavior.

My mother packed up the car with all my belongings, and on the drive home she was asking me many questions. But I only slumped into the passenger seat, while driving down the road. I was unable to speak, mute with depression. This really scared my mother, sitting in the car with the same daughter who screamed "I am going to become famous!" just months before. Who was this daughter who would change so drastically from one state of mind to another? It was time for the true diagnosis.

I was taken to the psychiatrist at the local mental health center. The same beautiful woman who had prescribed Stelazine was once again in front of me. It was then that Dr. Salina said "This is what I was afraid of: the depression and mania. Your daughter has a mental illness called Manic-Depression. She needs to be in a psychiatric hospital to get the help that she needs. Would you rather that she went up to Cleveland or to the local St. Joseph Riverside Hospital where they have a psychiatric ward?" My mother didn't take long to make the decision. She didn't want her daughter so far away, so I was to go to St. Joseph's Riverside Hospital located in Warren, Ohio.

First time in the Psychiatric Hospital

When the time came to be admitted, I was very fearful and not ready to trust anyone in the hospital setting. My mother kept telling me that I would get well if I just told the psychiatrist everything so that he could figure out the right treatment for me. She kept reassuring me that everything would be okay and that they would help me out of the depression once I was in the hospital. I was put into a wheelchair and was being pushed around the hospital by a young volunteer that they called a "candy striper" at that time. She was wheeling me to the psychiatric ward—or so I thought.

There I was, crying and hunched over in the wheelchair in great fear of what was going to happen, when the worst possible scenario took place. I was wheeled into a room filled with three other women who were lying on gurneys. A nurse standing nearby said to my mother, "Oh, my, she must be in terrible pain," to which she answered, "No, my daughter is depressed!" "Well, there must be some mistake. We are getting ready to prep her for surgery. Isn't she here to get her appendix out?" My mother explained that I was supposed to be going to the psychiatric ward and not to get my appendix out. The volunteer had made a mistake since the hospital was expecting two intakes; one for depression and the other for appendicitis. I was so upset I spilled out every swear word I could think of and more! My worst fears were coming to pass. Even the hospital couldn't help me. Suicide again poured through my thoughts and I wanted to just get up and run out of there. Fortunately, the mistake was taken care of and I was placed in a room on the psychiatric floor of the hospital where I belonged. Lying in bed that first night was such a relief because I had been given a shot to calm my anxiety. It was a good sleep that I hadn't had in months. In the morning I would be introduced to the psychiatrist and all would be well. There was something else troubling me too at the time. I was afraid that I was pregnant.

Dr. Radeem introduced himself early the next morning. I was intrigued by this tiny man from a foreign country who was there to give me help. He smiled and reassured me that I would be okay now. He explained to me that I was wearing pink sunglasses when I was manic and black sunglasses when I was depressed. His accent was strong and hard to understand, but he gave me peace and hope as he explained what I had been experiencing in his own analogies. It was truly a happy day of depression when I was introduced to Dr. Radeem. He promised he would take care of me and there was nothing to worry about anymore. My fear of being pregnant was also relieved when I found that the doctor did a test for that and he convinced me that I wasn't pregnant. That fear was alleviated at least. Dr. Radeem then gave me strong counsel that I should never allow myself to get pregnant. He convinced me that I would end up having a deformed baby because of the medication I was now on or, worse yet, my child would end up with mental illness just like me. I listened intently and because of this psychiatrist I gave up all hope of ever giving birth to a child.

I was moved into a room with three other women. It was a large room with four beds. That is when I met Jenna. Dr. Radeem encouraged me to get to know Jenna because she had the same diagnosis and could explain it even better first-hand. Jenna was much older than I, as were most all the patients, and I classified her as quite strange but friendly. I met many others during my first stay at St. Joe's. Some of them scared me while others were soothing. There was Susan. She was a very overweight lady with burn scars all over her face and arms. She turned to me and said, before I could even ask her a question, "I poured gasoline on myself and then lit myself on fire." I was shocked and quietly answered, "I'm so glad that you didn't die." Susan answered, "I'm not! I'm disappointed in myself!"

Then there were the two worst patients, Thad and Terry. Thad was an African American man with a very large stomach who chased after me when the others weren't looking. He made me very nervous and so I tried my best to stay far away from him. Terry, on the other hand was a very little man, extremely mentally ill. He would walk down the hallway and suddenly lift his right leg and say "No way, no way, no way!" This was something that he did repeatedly and I thought it was quite comical.

Although I thought that I was knowledgeable about a lot of things, I had actually lived a quite sheltered life. Some of the men were very manic and told jokes and laughed together on into the night. I felt that everyone was really old in comparison to me, which was probably true. I was looking for someone my own age to hang out with when I spotted a man lying in a bed with the door open. I peered into his room and thought he wasn't that old, but why was he lying so still and not waking up? This went on day after day.

I asked Dr. Radeem about Gerald, the man who lies in bed day after day and doesn't wake up. Dr. Radeem told me to be careful not to get too close to him when he does get up because he was not someone I needed to get to know. At the time I was so innocent and naive especially when it came to hard core drug users. When Gerald did get out of bed, I did not heed Dr. Radeem's words and I quickly tried to befriend Gerald. His mumbled words could not be understood the first time he came out of his room. He was sitting in the kitchen in a hospital gown when I came up and stated that I had been watching him as he lay day after day in his hospital bed. I was very curious to know what was wrong with Gerald. I was never told about his drug overdose nor would I have understood the horrors of heroin, cocaine, and other street drugs. Gerald did not scare me because he was so doped up he could not get his words out. I did realize that he was much older than me, and soon he found someone that he could relate to better—a woman by the name of Julie who was also in her late 20's or early 30's and had three adorable little girls. I became jealous of their relationship even though I let Julie borrow my clothes. My mother would come to visit me every day and warned me, "Nancy, if you were not in this situation you would never be jealous of Julie and Gerald." I agreed.

I enjoyed the activities that the psych ward offered. Bowling, crafts, relaxation exercises, patients' show and tell, and even long walks outside. Although I was in the psych ward, I got a wonderful suntan that summer, partly due to the medicine and partly due to the fact that we were allowed to sit outside in the back courtyard. There was such a sense of relief and peace that came with seeing Dr.

41

Radeem every day. He knew just the right words to say and made me feel so very taken care of.

The first few days were so comforting that I couldn't tell if I was depressed or not. Without really paying attention, I was swallowing several pills in the morning, afternoon and evening. I did not know what they were but I was very happy to be able to sleep the whole night through. There was a little loud speaker in every room and each morning a voice would say, "It's 7:00 o'clock, time to get dressed and get ready for breakfast." I didn't always want to get up at that time, but I knew it was what was expected of me. So I would get up, brush my teeth, and eat breakfast, and then it was time for morning exercise and a prayer led by Sister Marcy, a nun. I loved doing the morning stretches but rarely stayed for the prayer. After all, there was no God. If there was, then Dr. Radeem would not have told me that the night of my visitation and knowledge of fame was *not* reality. He said it was something called "a delusion of grandeur". That was very disappointing to hear. I would sometimes go back and forth with it in my mind. Do I believe God or do I believe a psychiatrist? At that point in time I didn't know the difference between the two. It was long before I heard the joke: "What is the difference between God and a psychiatrist? Answer: "God doesn't think he is a psychiatrist." Sister Marcy called me into her office one day to talk. I was eager to hear what she had to say as, being a nun; maybe she had some special knowledge that would help me in some way. Instead, Sister Marcy scolded me. She told me that I used my illness as a cover-up to stay away from true responsibility, or something of that nature. I did not understand what she meant, but it hurt my feelings. Did she have any idea how much I had suffered?

That first stay in the psychiatric ward was quite an eye-opening experience for me. Little did I know at the time that there would be many, many more hospitalizations in the future.

Where Do I Go From Here?

Living with my parents again, I was asked if I wanted to go back to college. My father basically made the decision for me to return to Kent State University, but I would go to the local branch which was not very far from our home in Cortland. He really wanted me to finish the courses that I had withdrawn from at the main campus so that the tuition wouldn't be wasted. I was feeling better, more stable, and so I took on the challenge. I was not sure what my major would be, so I just kept taking classes after I fulfilled the ones that I had withdrawn from. I took a drama class and found that I really liked to act on stage where I could be another character instead of myself. I also enjoyed Art Appreciation where I wrote a compelling comparative of mental illness and artists. I received an A on that paper and the teacher commented on my insight. I would always have a love for Art, English and French. I tried a class in Journalism, thinking that maybe I would go into that field. However, when I took a test and one of the questions was "What United States newspaper uses color images instead of black and white?" I bombed the answer, although USA Today was delivered to my parents' house on a daily basis. That took away my desire to be a journalist.

I loved making speeches although I had had to withdraw from my speech class at Kent State University. My last speech at the main campus had been on tornadoes, but because I was so anxious and depressed I had ripped up the written speech. But then I decided to deliver it anyway, stating that a tornado had demolished my hand written pages! Now, at Kent Branch and feeling much better, I was able to deliver a speech on Manic-Depression and what I was going through with the illness. Several students commented on what guts it must have taken to admit that fact to everybody in the class. I had read an "Ann Landers" letter about a college boy who seemed to have it all, including being a star football player, but he committed suicide. His mother wrote the article warning others about an illness called manic-depression. She stated, "If only we had known that he was suffering from this mental illness, we could have saved him." I read this article to the class. It was just a taste of what was to become a lifelong passion of educating people about mental illness.

I made friends with yet another "Christian" girl who informed me that prior to her getting married, her parents made sure she was home at midnight every night. I thought that was absolutely crazy as I would stay out until 2:00 or 3:00 AM. I liked her because she was straightforward about what it was like to be a true born-again Christian, but I didn't like her judgment. When I told her that my boyfriend and I had spent the night at a hotel, I remember her saying, "Shame on you!" You can imagine how badly I took this "scolding." "I hate Christians!" I remember saying over and over. I truly thought that Christians believed that they were better than the average person because they lived "Right" and everyone else lived "Wrong." Never would I EVER imagine that I would ever become a born-again Christian myself. No way!

I began taking the courses to fulfill an Associate's Degree in Business. I had dropped my typing class in high school due to the depression, so I found myself taking Beginners, Intermediate and finally Advanced Typewriting. Because of this second depression I nearly didn't pass Beginners but slid past with a "D." It just seemed so hard for my fingers to figure out where all the keys were. The next step was to take courses like "Intro to Word Processing." Yes, in the early "80's," word processing is what using a computer was called. The computers were very large at that time taking up half of a room each. Information was saved on large square things called "Floppy disks." I was going to take shorthand but was told that it was becoming obsolete, which it was. I made many friends at Kent Branch and had a good time going to school there. I was set to graduate in 1985 but needed one more class: economics. I took the class while I worked full time as a secretary called a Kelly Girl at Warren Assembly, the Ravene plant.

I soon became more and more interested in a man at the plant, my supervisor, Bill, who was 20 years my senior. Being manic opened many forbidden doors and having an affair with a married man was just one of them. It was a really bad choice to dabble in this serious relationship but the excitement of it was too much to pass up. I will never forget the first time I kissed Bill, this tall lanky man with grey hair. I knew right after our lips touched that I was in deep trouble. "I shouldn't have done that!" I said over and over to myself. But the temptation was so very great. Bill was a much respected man at work, and it gave me a real high whenever I would see him. At the time, I never worried about his wife finding out, or even his three children, for that matter, Bill actually had a 19-year-old son who had a drug problem and two younger children that he adored. He told me that his wife didn't understand him. He always said that I was the greatest, most beautiful woman he had ever met. (At least that is what he told me.) He also was into something called "New Age" and he gave me a book about it. As much as I read it and tried to understand what he was talking about, I never really could grasp the concepts of it, which was okay with him. He still was crazy about me. The mania had taken over and the consequences were not as much an issue. Soon it became more than just a rumor at the Ravene plant that Bill and I were hooking up. At the time, I did not care what anyone said: I would do as I pleased. Bill was 41 years old and I was 21. He seemed to me to be in great shape for his age. I jumped into this relationship full force and looked only to Bill as I idolized every word he said to me. He was so wise and OLD.

It was all about that time, as I reached my 21st birthday, that my father suggested that I move to Rhode Island where my two sisters and their husbands lived. My father thought that the economy was better in Rhode Island and that I could get a good job. All this was true, but I had to leave Bill behind. I was in disgrace but did not care or know better. A new chapter of my life was beginning in East Greenwich, RI, but I was never able to leave behind the dreaded mania and depression. I had come to believe that I WAS a manic-depressive, and it defined me.

Chapter 5

The Move to Rhode Island

I saw an ad for a Manic Depressive Support Group in Boston and quickly called and joined the group which was located at McClain Hospital and held once a week. It was a large support group with a president who was a postman. There were some wonderful people in this group and they helped me a lot. One older woman had a bumper sticker on her car that said "Honk if you're on Lithium!"

In Rhode Island, I made my home with my sister Gini and her husband Larry. I got a job within a month at a National Bank in downtown Providence. With the help of my sisters I learned how to drive in the heart of the city and park in an all-day parking lot every day. I worked for the Corporate Real Estate Department which was on the first floor of a beautiful 26-story skyscraper, typing up million dollar loans for the rich who mainly built condominiums with an ocean view.

While living in Rhode Island I was continually searching, searching for a man to fill my empty heart. Suicidal and insecure, I ran through a number of dates looking for the answer to my emotional distress. None of them had any answers for me and it's a wonder I am still alive because of all the risks I took with strangers. When I would realize that no one could help me out of this mind set, I would sit in solitude in despairing pain agonizing over whom to go to next. Most of the men that I met were initially attracted to me but found that my personality was lacking stability. Either I showed only the face of excitement, or else the dark truth would pour from my lips, letting out my ugly secrets. I was being tortured by evil and I wasn't even aware of it. Alcohol was both a friend and a foe, and I drank when taking all sorts of medicine. How my heart would skip beats and pound hard when I lay in bed with the bedroom ceiling spinning out of control!

Where was my sanity? It seemed to me to be an unusual process, this manic-depressive cycle repeating and repeating itself, loaded with sorrow for four to five months, then again uplifted into a manic state for a shorter amount of time. Why couldn't I see the truth back then? I was blinded by the overwhelming feelings of never ending hopelessness, tormenting me, eating me alive. Crying was continual. The tears would pour out of my eyes. The sobbing was ceaseless; my entire body was racked with convulsing, jerks and screams. The sorrow was throughout every portion of my being.

Woe to me, a strange person who differed from the rest. Even upon meeting another tortured soul, I still felt distant. Alone. Looking in the mirror, I tried to hide myself under make-up and flowing blonde curls. With a glance others could see the beauty of a young woman brandishing an insane smile. "Please be my friend." "Hold me in your arms until I melt into a puddle of muddy water." "Curse me 'til I die." "Hurt me where it already hurts." "Cuddle me dead." "Empty the last of my personhood." "Pleasure me with lies." SORROW.

One snowy morning I woke up with a start. I jumped out of bed with a feeling of dreaded doom in my heart concerning Bill. I went to the telephone and called the long distant number to my friend Lana who worked at the Ravene plant. Before I could say a word, Lana yelled into the phone "Nancy, Bill's son is dead! Bill found him dead this morning in his bed. They think it was an accidental overdose!" My mind could hardly accept what Lana was saying as my thoughts went to Bill and how horrified he must have felt to find his son dead like that. I wanted to call Bill so badly but knew that I couldn't call him at home. Suddenly, a wave of guilt flooded through my body. "Oh, if only Bill had spent more time with his son instead of spending every second away from home with me!" I cried and cried, believing that this was somehow my fault.

It wasn't long after that when Bill himself called me and told me that he had suffered a mild heart attack while working out with one of his friends. None the less, I really was feeling like I wanted to break it off totally with Bill. I was dating someone new in Rhode Island and I didn't have any feelings for him anymore. After I moved to Rhode Island all the excitement of dating a married man was gone completely.

I stopped taking his calls. Bill became more persistent. He was writing me long letters and calling me all the time. We didn't have caller ID so I would have my sister tell him that I wasn't home. Finally, one day, I did answer the phone and Bill alluded to some ideas he had written to me. He wanted to come visit me! I was stunned and did not know how to say "No." After all, the man had been through some really rough times lately, so I finally agreed. My sister and her husband told me that they would be totally uncomfortable if he stayed there at their home with them, so I picked a nice hotel and lived there for a week with Bill while going to work every day. He would show up at noon at the bank I worked at and take me out to lunch each day. It was embarrassing. Soon the rumors started at my NEW place of employment. Who was this older gentleman coming to take Nancy to lunch every day? I really did not like having him there. There was absolutely no attraction left and I didn't like living out of a suitcase. He also was hurting very much because of his son, and this pillar of strength, the supervisor at work, was showing me his most vulnerable side. But I was rude and thought about no one but myself in those days.

When I did take a trip back to Ohio, I went to visit my "friends" at the Ravene plant. Each and every one of them looked at me and sarcastically asked if I had visited the front office yet. They ALL knew what had gone on between Bill and me, and now that Bill was getting a divorce, I looked and felt like a complete heathen.

Although I had started out on the wrong foot by being overly friendly to the men and women working at the bank—(try going to New England and see how friendly they are to newcomers)—in time I made a few friends with some girls at the bank. Meanwhile, my sister and I decided it was time for me to live on my own, no longer interrupting the lives of her and her husband. One day, prior to moving out of my sister's house, I got a really bad case of bronchitis. Being a smoker, I had this extremely deep cough that almost sounded like a dog barking. I called work and told them I was sick. Well, Gini worked the afternoon shift and had something really crazy in mind for us to do that day. She talked me into going to the beach. We went to the beach almost every weekend in the summer, so I told her I guess it might be good for my bronchitis to lay out in the beautiful sunshine. This was a new beach we had never gone to before and it was called "Moonstone." As we drove down the highway toward the ocean, Gini explained that we were headed for no ordinary beach. I couldn't figure out what she was talking about but noticed that once we got to the beach parking lot, we had to walk a long way to get to the particular beach she wanted to go to. When it seemed we had walked a few miles people began appearing in view. People were sunbathing. People who were…oh dear God! NAKED! My sister and I were on a nude beach and I was mortified. We put our towels down in the sand and lay down on our stomachs. Gini, who always was a bit of an exhibitionist, was embarrassed too, but mostly because of my cough. She called it an "elephant mating call" and forbid me to cough because it attracted too much attention. Each time I lit up a cigarette and took a puff, I would start with this barking cough again and attracted *more* attention. Gini hated smoking anyway and would try to grab the cigarette out of my hand. Ever since then I have called my sister J-Bird and she kids me about my "elephant mating call." We still joke to this day about that memorable adventure to Moonstone beach although I don't think I would have even considered going there had it not been for Gini.

When it was time for me to move out on my own, I was a little bit nervous but made friends with this girl named Maggie who was a true blue party girl. What I mean by that was—Maggie did drugs and drank a lot, although she was very quiet and kind of shy. At first I wasn't aware of her doing drugs, but I did notice that she could drink like a fish and often got sick in the morning. We became instant friends and decided to move in together. It was a first time of living on our own for both of us, knowing that we were entirely in charge of paying the rent and other bills. We decided not to buy any food at first so that we could figure out how much money we had between us. The house was in Cranston, RI. It was the bottom floor of a three story apartment house. I had purchased a water bed and Maggie and I bought furniture from some friends. It seemed like the ideal set-up and she and I had a lot of fun until the depression took over once again. All of the emotional pain began running its course overtaking my mind as I tried to explain the illness to Maggie. Maggie did not understand it at all; in fact, she seemed not to believe me, especially when I told her I was feeling suicidal because of it. She was putting on a false "nice" act to my face but talked smack behind my back. I didn't realize this until I started hearing from everyone we knew, from the owner of the local store to our landlord; to each and every person Maggie worked with that she lived with a girl who was raving mad. My feelings were more than hurt as the depression cut through my heart with every negative word I heard about myself.

Meanwhile, I was seeing this less-than-professional psychiatrist who used to flirt with me and insisted that I call him Marvin (his first name) instead of his real name. Because I got so dressed up for work and then came to see him after work, he did not see the severity of my manic-depression until I nearly ended my life. I begged him to put me in the psychiatric hospital, but "Dr." Marvin didn't think I belonged there. He told me I was too good to fit in with "all those weirdoes." Yes, a psychiatrist who called mental patients "weirdoes," hard to believe! He had not yet gotten the records from Ohio and had no proof that I had been hospitalized before several times. I told him that I had a gun. Finally, "Dr." Marvin wrote up the papers for me to go into the hospital. It seemed that I was more afraid of what I might do to myself than he was.

Butler Hospital, Providence, RI

Butler Hospital on beautiful Blackstone Boulevard was definitely a high class mental hospital. The tree-lined boulevard wound up to a large driveway area where the stately building stood, looking more like an upscale museum than a place for the "insane".

I believe that there were four floors to the hospital and each floor had a level of severity according to the patients there. When I unpacked my suitcase, the staff went through everything I had brought with me looking for a sharp object or anything else that a person could hurt themselves with. This was standard procedure even at St. Joe's Riverside. I looked down regretfully at my tennis shoes when the staff person insisted that I take off my shoelaces. As at St. Joe's, a nurse took my hairdryer, curling iron and make-up and I would have to ask for it each time I needed to use any of these items. It always seemed like such a long wait for a nurse to go in the back, find what I needed and finally give it to me.

I quickly realized that at Butler when a person is suicidal they took more precautionary measures then I was accustomed to. Each time I used the bathroom, the door had to be kept partially open and a staff person stood outside waiting for any type of negative behavior on my behalf. I couldn't understand what I could be doing wrong as even the mirrors in the bathroom were the wavy kind made out of something other than glass. It reminded me of going to a fair and seeing the mirrors that made a person look mighty thin or mighty large. I had a difficult time putting my make-up on using these mirrors. When I would finally agree to take a shower, again, the door had to be partially open for the staff member. I sang as loud as I could in the shower hoping the nurse would be too busy listening to my song to stare at my naked body. There was absolutely no privacy. It seemed as though there was someone assigned to each and every suicidal patient to keep watch on them 24 hours a day. That is why it was such a shock… and so very unlikely… for an event of extreme horror to erupt as it did suddenly early one morning.

I was lying on my bed in my assigned room when I heard a gunshot. I rolled over to look outside my door and saw flashing lights and heard a recorded voice saying "Go to your rooms." "Go to your rooms." Then there was extreme pandemonium. The nurses, doctors, and everyone else working at that time were running around in a complete frenzy. Not knowing what exactly was happening, I lay there listening. As far as I could tell, someone had done the unimaginable. Could it be that someone shot themselves right there in a hospital room? The answer would come soon enough. I could hear the staff yelling "Oh my God!" "Oh my God!" It was apparent what had happened. I thought to myself: *the lucky son-of-a-gun!* After everyone came back to the nurses' station and the flashing lights stopped completely, I went out and stood by the nurses' station to listen to their stories. The nurses seemed to be traumatized. The one male nurse, still in shock, was talking about seeing this man's brains splattered against the wall. The man had brought his gun in his pants and that is why it went undetected. Although he was going into the hospital for help, he had successfully completed suicide. I was not frightened by this; I was not horrified by this. I just wished it had been me who had the guts to have shot myself.

I was constantly taking medication and was now meeting with a doctor named Dr. Thomas who seemed to take a quick judgmental dislike to me because I spoke to men more than to women. He told me that I had two different personality disorders. One disorder concerned my relationship with men. The second concerned my inability to keep a job for over a year, which he called a work personality disorder. This just made me feel worse about myself and he never bothered to explain what that meant. When I saw Dr. Thomas and wanted to hear encouraging words like Dr. Radeem used to say, he would only say detrimental things like "It says on your chart that you talked to this man for 20 minutes." I could not understand why that was so important. Men were safe, as far as I was concerned. They were quick to tell me everything I wanted to hear. If I was a beauty than it wouldn't matter as much that deep down I felt like I was not worthy to walk the earth.

I changed rooms several times and now had a roommate. She was a beautiful blonde young lady named Julie, older than myself. Julie and I didn't talk but we both went to bed early, around 7:00 PM. It made me feel good to go to sleep with a roommate like Julie. It was a reminder of growing up with my sister, Linda, in the room with me. Poor Julie had her left wrist wrapped up tightly with several layers of gauge. I didn't ask, but was pretty certain that Julie had attempted suicide by cutting her wrist.

There were four women who were called "the anorectics." They walked around slowly like little toothpick silhouettes with their rib cages sticking out predominately. They were kind of scary looking and reminded me of the Holocaust concentration camp-type people. All I could think of was: why would anyone starve themselves to death? I couldn't understand it. These four ladies were not allowed to eat with the rest of us. Just as I was being monitored on suicide watch, these ladies would go into the kitchen, and each and every morsel of food that was swallowed would be monitored. They would take a very long time to eat, and sometimes all the encouraging in the world would not make these women eat. One of the anorectic women was Anna. Anna had grown up on the sandy beaches of Cape Cod. She was extremely depressed and weighed a mere 80 pounds. She was very friendly, though, and soon Anna and I became friends. Anna told me that her doctor, Dr. Roberts had warned her that if she did not eat even a piece of fruit, they would feed her intravenously though a needle in her hand. I thought that was quite drastic and asked Anna if she was going to start eating. Anna said "No way!" Soon Anna started walking around with an IV drip in her hand with some brown stuff in a bag. It looked pretty gross to me but must have been full of nutrients. I was truly amazed that even this uncomfortable IV did not make her decide to eat.

Later, when I was hospitalized for the third time at Butler Hospital, I met up with Anna again. We also kept in touch by phone calls and letters. Anna was a good friend to me. One of the most amazing things that showed our bond occurred when Anna went through a series of electric shock therapy. I was warned by a nurse that each time Anna was shocked that she would come back not remembering who she was, where she was, or what had been done to her. I was waiting for Anna after one such shock treatment. They wheeled Anna on a gurney into her room and I went into the room and waited for her to wake up. I always felt bad for Anna because of the glue in her pretty blonde hair that took a long time to wash out. Anna still had the electrodes on her head when she slowly awoke from the anesthesia. She looked at me and said "Hi, Nancy." It was amazing that she could remember me. There was a strong connection between the two of us, and I used to ask her "How can anyone who grew up in a town like Cape Cod ever be depressed?"

I was discharged from the hospital after a lengthy stay and went straight back to work as a secretary.

Chapter 6

The Horrors of the Illness

Honestly, to me, it would never have mattered what the name of this "illness" was. To me, it was an all-consuming raging fire that took everything from me and left me with internal ashes. From the very moment I woke up in the morning until I slept again I would have the most negative, frightening, horrid thoughts 24 hours a day, seven days a week, for months and months on end. There seemed to be no hope and no ability to function as a human being. During those low times, I breathed death. In and out, I would lie in bed listening to my breathing. In and out. Will this insane 'life support' just stop? Please? In and out. God gave my breath. Air. I hated God for that. I was too young and too healthy. As I listened to my breathing, I asked, "Why did the next breath always come back in?" Death was the only thought that soothed me. *What was this joke called Life?* I would ask repeatedly. And so it went. There was never any answer for the pain I was in.

Then, out of the clear blue sky, I would wake up one morning so unexpectedly full of excitement. I would leap out of bed so happy to be alive, run into the bathroom, splash water on my face, look in the mirror and see my own eyes. They were dancing! From that moment forward, usually for two to three months, I would engage in activity that was uncharacteristic of me. It was also embarrassing and, at times, detrimental to my own wellbeing.

To me, it was usually wonderful at first. Who wouldn't want to feel as though they could do anything competently? I was so sure that I was going to become famous in Hollywood that three times in my life I saved up enough money for a plane ticket. I wanted to be a movie star, or at least have my own TV show! The last time I did this, I decided to consult with my father. When I rounded the corner of my father's office at work, he looked at me in surprise! I had never been to his office before. I sat down and told him my plan to fly to Hollywood and become a famous actress. My father, refocusing his eyes from his work and on to his "crazy daughter" showing up with the news of my newest manic delusion, was at first speechless. There may have been a hint of amusement in my father's eyes, but he took me seriously because he knew how serious I was. My father talked me out of it, for now. It was a bad decision. My dream of being on Johnny Carson was slowly vanishing as Johnny Carson was getting too old to be on his own show. I still could never figure out how this fame would come about, but each time I was manic these thoughts and ideas would resurface. How was this fame going to happen and why? By playing the trumpet? Singing? Acting? It just <u>was</u> going to happen. I knew it and God knew it. It was those blasted psychiatrists who got in the way with their term "delusion of grandeur." That term was ridiculous to me when I was manic. Nobody but *nobody* could tell me I was wrong about anything when I was in that state of mind; especially when it had to do with my own destiny.

Max

Partying was one of my favorite things to do and the place to be was "Shabooms!" It was a 50's nightclub in downtown Providence that actually had a bright red car set up in the middle where the DJ sat and played all the oldies. Sometimes, this bar was so crowded that it became standing room only. I made friends with some girls at the bank and we would all go out for drinks and dancing. Although I was on psychotropic medication, drinking white or black Russians were an every weekend affair. Men would buy my drinks and smoking was allowed back then, so it was: alcohol, cigarettes and men, in that order. There didn't seem to be any problem with hanging out with men, but as far as having a long lasting relationship—that seemed impossible because of my changing moods. I really didn't want anyone to know just how bad I felt about myself, but even with my big smile, it would always become apparent to a man that there was definitely something wrong with my mind. That was when the person I met would say goodbye, and I would feel the rejection envelope my mind and my soul. I used to wonder who could ever fall in love with me when I didn't love myself. It was quite a surprise to me when it finally did happen.

I was dancing on the Shaboom's dance floor when I caught the eye of a gentleman standing on the side of the dance floor. He looked to me like Burt Reynolds in his heyday. His eyes were transfixed on me dancing and I decided to go talk to him. His name was Max. We started talking and I soon found out that Max had been in the military, but had just returned to his hometown of Providence. We had an interesting conversation and there was definitely an instant attraction between the two of us. I invited him to my apartment afterwards where we talked well into the night, and Max slept over on the couch. At the time Max was working in sales and had just moved back in with his mother on the East side. He was 22 years old and I was 23. Max then decided to move in with Maggie and me, and it all happened very quickly. I had never met anyone quite like him. He was so into electronics that he took apart my beloved typewriter until it was nothing but keys sticking out, and then put the whole thing back together just for fun. Max was also going to school to get an IT type of job. He was at the top of his class with hard work and natural intelligence. I felt myself fall madly in love, and Max did the same. We were very happy together.

In time, I decided one night that it was a perfect opportunity to explain my deep dark secret to Max. I wondered what he would think of me after I told him about the manic-depression. It was always a risk to tell someone about this illness that had been running my life for years. I sat on the floor of my bedroom waiting patiently for Max to come in the room to talk about it. Max seemed preoccupied with something he was doing in the kitchen. I was very nervous and was trying to think of the best way to explain it so he wouldn't be too shocked. "Let's see, I thought. " Should I just tell him I have a problem with depression? That wouldn't cause too much shock." Instead, Max had a shock for me! As I looked into Max's brown eyes I thought I saw a tear. Amazingly enough, I really was seeing a tear roll down his face and I hadn't yet uttered a word!

As soon as I began my explanation of the mental problem, he stopped me and whispered with his voice cracking, "I already know." "You already know what?" I asked. "I already know what you're going to tell me." I was surprised to say the least, but before I could even register how he could have found out, Max explained. "I had a dream one night and it seemed so real. I dreamt that I had fallen in love with a beautiful young girl and we were just right for each other. Then the dream turned into horror as this girl that I loved committed suicide. When I saw you on the dance floor that night at Shabooms, I knew it was you. I knew that I have to save you from committing suicide. By this point, Max was really crying and I just sat amazed. Then he said he had something else to share with me. The reason that he came back to Rhode Island so soon was because of a problem he had gone through with the military. He hated coming back to Providence to start his life over, but he didn't have a choice. After all of this was said, Max stopped crying and we went to bed.

I started having a mood change from depression to mania. This process began slowly but turned into a full blown out-of-reality break. I had stopped taking my medications. Max moved back with his mother during this period of time because he couldn't handle my out-of-control behavior. I t was extremely scary.. I was thinking that my brother-in-law killed my sister and was telling Maggie all about it while crying hysterically. Maggie was shocked and started to cry too, believing it to be true also. I had totally lost my mind.

58

Maggie called my two sisters and they and their husbands showed up at the apartment. Maggie was surprised that my one sister was okay. I had no idea that they had called an ambulance when I stripped off my clothes and stood naked in front of everyone yelling "Look at the body god gave me." I also said some horrible things to my sisters, believing that my sister Chris would bear the next Messiah. Someone finally made me get dressed as an EMT walked in the front door. I exclaimed "What a beautiful specimen of a man!" The next thing I remembered was being taken away inside an ambulance with my sister Gini at my side. The man in the ambulance was wearing all white and I was sure that he was the Pillsbury Dough Boy. He had a pretty big belly so I kept poking him in the stomach waiting for him to giggle like the Pillsbury Dough Boy on the commercials. I then told him that he ate at McDonald's too much and that was why he was fat. Gini later told me that I destroyed this man's watch as I thought it was evil. The ambulance arrived at Rhode Island Hospital where I was wheeled into a room and put on a gurney. I was yelling and screaming and not wanting to lie down. The adrenaline along with the mania was too much for the staff there to handle. Suddenly four big men showed up and I watched in horror as they tied me down with leather straps. First my left arm, my left leg at the ankle area and then my right arm and leg. As hard as I tried to wiggle out of them, I could not budge the straps. I kept on screaming and trying to scare people with my "low demonic voice." I wanted them to think that I was possessed by the devil.

My sisters explained that I was taking lithium at the time, and when a person came in take blood to check my level, I fought hard not to let her put the needle into my arm. When the doctor came in I spoke in my low demonic voice and told him that if he didn't go get a hairbrush and brush my hair that he would have a heart attack and die that very night. The doctor actually did as he was told and came back with a hairbrush…and also a shot. There were a few nurses around and while this doctor who seemed afraid of me started brushing my hair, one of the nurses jammed the shot into my arm before I had a chance to protest. The shot was something pretty powerful and I could feel it penetrate my mind and body. Soon I was slurring my words. Just then, a roommate was wheeled into the room. It was obvious that this woman was drunk because the entire room suddenly reeked of alcohol. I noticed that the woman was extremely thin just like the "anorectics" on the psych floor I had met. "What is your name?" I asked. "Nancy" the drunken woman replied. I told her that Nancy was my name also and that it meant, "Grace." "Nancy and Nancy" carried on a pathetic conversation. Nancy was drunk out of her mind and I was mentally out of my mind. What a pair. My sisters and brothers-in-law one by one came in to see me. I begged them to take the restraints off but they all said that they could not do it. "Please untie me, Gini." "I love you," was all that she could say hiding her tears.

The next thing I remembered was waking up in Butler Hospital on Blackstone Boulevard once again. I was very surprised to see my roommate from the emergency room there. When I saw Nancy I realized that she really was one of the "the anorectics." My psychotic mind told me that Nancy and I would merge into one person so that Nancy would get some nourishment. When I went downstairs in line for the cafeteria, I made sure to eat plenty of vegetables, even ones that I didn't like, so that Nancy would get some of my solid food in her stomach. Upon arriving back to the ward, I noticed Nancy and the other anorectics had not eaten in the kitchen yet. Nancy told me that she was very hungry because they had not gotten their trays yet. I told her not to be concerned and it was okay because "I ate for the both of us."

One of the interesting things about being in a psychotic state is the memory of it does not come back until a later date. Not only that but all the strange mind games that go on while in a psychiatric ward are dulled by the amount of antipsychotic drugs that a person takes every few hours of every day. This particular stay in the hospital was memorable in several ways. I was lying in bed one day and staring at the light above my head. I, in my mind, was not allowed to take my eyes off of the light in my room or something bad would happen. I could hear the television set out in the common area. The news was on and there was a special bulletin that a tornado had gone through

Rhode Island. At this point I was sure that it was the end of the world. I lay there unable to move a muscle—full of fear. The thought of the world ending at any second made my heart beat out of my chest. There normally were absolutely no tornadoes in Rhode Island, only hurricanes! It was so scary that I decided I *had* to get out of my bed and out with the other patients. I came across this little old man sitting in a chair watching television. I tried to speak to him, to let him know that he was very lucky to be old because the end of the world was at hand. It was like any second could be the end. My voice trailed off as the old man looked straight ahead with no expression. There were just too many drugs in my system to speak.

One day while sitting on a couch, I noticed a tall young man with very dark hair and dark eyes. I asked him what his name was and he said "If you really want to know the truth, I am God." I said "THE God?" He replied "Yes." I was mesmerized by this man. I believed his delusion of being God as much as he did! I had some profound conversations with this man. He told me, "The people living on earth are so very selfish that they believe there are no other galaxies. People on earth are so unaware that there are many earths with many types of people. It bothers me that earthlings believe that this is all there is. Why would I only make one planet for people to live?" I thought that comment was very interesting. This man who claimed to be God also said "Nancy, if you ever need some money, like some change or anything, there is a cup located at the nurses' station and whatever is in it, it is for you." I asked this man if he loved me since I had often heard people say "God loves you." He said he loved everyone and he gave me a kiss on the lips. Just at that moment, Max walked up, since it was visiting hours and he had decided to come back into my life. I was very embarrassed and said, "Don't worry, Max, this man is God. Of course I would kiss him!"

Days later, I went up to the nurses' station and began searching for a cup. Lo and behold, there it was. A little white paper cup that I knew was left for me. I picked up the cup and in it was some change but also a beautiful blue Catholic saint charm for a necklace or bracelet. I, not knowing anything about Catholicism, took the charm and hid it until I got out of the psychiatric hospital and bought a chain at a local store to make it a necklace.

I had been taking this medication called lithium since my first hospitalization in 1980. At this point Dr. Thomas was giving me an extra high dosage of 1800 mg to try to get me to come down from the mania. The dosage made me feel very ill as it was above therapeutic levels. I was also taking Haldol in a high dose which made me slur my speech so badly that it was difficult for others to understand what I was saying.

Upon being discharged from the hospital, I returned to work only to realize that my manic episode had been in full gear while I was working before the hospital stay.

Once my brother-in-law Keith had come and escorted me out of the bank in an attempt to help me get the help I needed.

The memory came back. I had sat in the chair next to my supervisor Greg's desk prior to hospitalization and said, "Greg...I love you." The look on Greg's face was something that I could look back and laugh at. Greg had been told by the Vice President to "take me under his wing." Which he had and he really helped me keep my job. I was very grateful to have a boss like Greg. He was patient and kind to me and did not belittle me in any way like the other folks who worked in the Corporate Real Estate department had. I had some close friends but the others had shunned me from the beginning. Some of them called me "Ellie Mae" from the TV show The Beverly Hillbillies. They believed that I was from some other planet called Ohio and did not fit in with the native New Englanders. I still struggled with my emotions concerning men from the past and men in the present. Max was definitely the most wonderful gift that could have come into my life, but I was so troubled that my heart still ached for Bill (the married man), and now for Max.

The time soon came when the mania subsided and depression reared its ugly head once again. This time the bank was not so forgiving when I was put back into Butler Hospital and a letter came in the mail that I was discharged from my job position. However, the bank allowed me to keep my insurance for one year. The news was broken to me by my brother-in-law, Keith, who thought I would be upset. Interestingly enough, I did not care that I was let go.

Chapter 7

Providence to Denver with a Miracle in between

Our one year lease was up so Maggie and I parted ways, and Max and I moved into an apartment in Providence located at the top of Federal Hill. We lived in the upstairs of a house and the landlord and his family lived downstairs. Although the area was considered Italian, the landlord and his wife and children were Polish. It was easy to hear what they were saying downstairs, and sometimes we could hear the father yelling and swearing. Before moving away, Max and I went to a polka dance with the landlord and his family where he showed me how to do the one-two-three polka.

During the time of living in Providence with Max, I suffered with depression so badly that I would stay in bed for long stretches of time. The only work that I would do was secretarial work through a temporary agency. That way I would not feel guilty for leaving my jobs which was a habit I had gotten into over the years of suffering with this mental illness. Sometimes I worked places while I was in depression, as was the case of a temporary job at a sewage worksite. My office was in a trailer and the job site was filled with men. I was actually the only woman there after the last secretary who trained me left. The insecurity was so strong during my tenure there that I became more and more intense with flirting and living on my young good looks. There were a lot of men who gave me attention at that time and it seemed to be the only way that I had any confidence in myself. The former secretary had been a very good one, or so the office men told me, and I felt like I would never live up to her reputation. Although the sewage employees had a dirty job, I stayed in a nice dry office inside the trailer and enjoyed my job time as much as could be expected.

Max was still going to school and working at a place called Staying Safe which was owned and operated by two men who seemed very pleased with his work. The main job was to install alarms into cars, but it was also a very dirty job and his clothes got filthy. Max would work until very late at night and would always come home smelling like marijuana, but he was so good to me that it didn't matter. He helped me anyway that he could.

Prior to moving to Providence, I had had a major suicide attempt. I was off work that day and feeling more suicidal than I ever had before. The thought of shooting myself in the head seemed like the only solution as I cried and cried so long and loud that I felt I was drowning in my own tears. Looking down at the hardwood floor, I pictured an ant speeding along under the wood. At that moment I truly believed that an ant had more importance than I did. It was overwhelmingly one of the worst moments of my life and I could only think of dying. I wanted to be dead and out of my misery. The depression was so strong. I cried so loud, I was wailing. Why was all this coming into my mind yet AGAIN? Death. Negative thoughts. Horrible thoughts. Thoughts turned into words inside my mind. "Nancy, you must shoot yourself in the head. You will be free of all pain. Do it, you loser! You are a worthless woman!" Without notice, the door swung open, and lo and behold, there was Max, home in the middle of the day which was very unusual. He saw the state that I was in and this time it scared him. The two of us went into the bedroom and Max stood holding onto me and then he fell to his knees. I turned my face upward and took a long deep breath as the tears rolled down my swollen face. "Oh God, help me!" I whispered. Then something amazing happened. It was another supernatural moment that would change my life forever.

As I stood there, even though I was not near a window, I felt these bright rays of sunlight pouring straight down on me. It was so strong that I closed my eyes as a warm blanket of love enveloped my whole body all the way to the bottom of my feet. Without knowing anything else, I knew it was Jesus. God had opened heaven for just a moment in time and I felt a deep love come upon me like no person on this earth could ever give. It was warm and Strong and true and Real. This love just penetrated me completely. It felt so good; I just wanted to stay in that position forever. Suddenly, still with my eyes closed, I felt the spirits of those who had passed away before me. There were many, but I mainly recognized my Grandmother McCurdy and my brother-in-law Keith's father, Charlie, who had both passed away. They were so happy, like a joyful welcoming committee into heaven. My spirit was ever so ready to join them as they all showed so much love and light. All at once I heard an audible voice which was in unison of the many spirits which said *"It's not your time yet!"* Their voices were loud and clear and full of power. As I opened my eyes the rays of sunlight left, the love left, the spirits left, and there I was standing in my bedroom with the depression falling right back on me, but not quite as strong. I looked down at Max and said "Did you hear that? What were you doing?" Max answered "I didn't know what to do for you, Nance, so I got on my knees and I prayed." I explained to him what had just happened to me as he helped me pack for the psychiatric ward. This was my third trip to Butler Hospital. Looking back, I realize that the dream that Max had right before we met had come to pass. He had stopped me from committing suicide!

Although this supernatural experience happened to me, I still felt no need to believe in or allow Jesus into my life. I still experienced the misery of depression and the elation of mania over and over during my lifetime.

It was during one of my manic psychotic episodes, when the phone rang in the middle of the night startling me awake. It was my brother-in-law in Maryland calling to tell me that my sister, Linda, had just given birth to their son, and they named him Justin. I was so excited because this was the first-born baby of any of my sisters. But what excited me even more was that I believed that Justin was the second Messiah. Later, as I talked to Linda, she said that everywhere they went, little Justin was looked upon as being a beautiful child. I felt that this was a confirmation that Justin was a 'holy child." It is an interesting phenomenon that people who become psychotic get religious ideas even if they have had no religious background prior to that. I spent a lifetime asking psychiatrists why that was. It was only later, after I converted to Christianity, that I realized that it was a ploy from the devil to make unbelievers think that believers in Jesus were all crazy. This is totally untrue.

One night, while living in Federal Hill in Providence with Max, I had a very significant dream. It was one of those dreams that I deeply felt was somehow extremely significant. I dreamt that I was on a bus, like a Greyhound. I was sitting near the back of the bus when it stopped and the bus driver stood up and announced "One way trip to Colorado!" I squirmed in my seat because I did not want to go to Colorado, I wanted to go back to Rhode Island or Ohio and be with my family. The bus driver quickly sat back down in his seat and the bus took off. Soon the squealing wheels of the bus stopped again and the bus driver stood up and said "All for Ohio!" in a loud booming voice. The doors of the bus opened and I leaped out of my seat and made my way down the aisle, very happy that I was going back to my home in Ohio. As I reached the front of the bus, the bus driver shut the doors and stood up, looked right past me like I wasn't even there, and shouted, "One way trip to Colorado!" I started to argue that I wanted to get off in Ohio, but the bus driver ignored my pleas. He sat back down in the driver's seat and the bus rolled on. I was filled with anxiety wanting nothing more than to get off this bus headed for Colorado. It seemed apparent to me in the dream that I would get to Colorado and never be able to leave since the driver kept repeating that it was only one way. I woke up from the dream shivering in fear.

It was not long after I had this nightmare when Max came to me and said "I really want to move to Colorado." I stood frozen. "Are you serious?" I asked, and began telling Max of the dream I had had. Max did not seem swayed in any way by this dream. He had been stationed in the service in Colorado and he believed it would be the ideal place to live. I was very confused. I didn't know if I should break-up with him to get out of moving or not. I wondered where I would live if I didn't go with him. After all, I loved Max and he was always so good to me. Max, who was normally a quiet man who kept his business to himself, had made a list of goals that he intended to implement as soon as he got to Colorado. His list of goals was not particularly long, but what was written I could tell was solid in his mind. He wanted to get a good job in electronics. He wanted to start eating right, with nutritious food instead of his favorite carrot cake every day. He wanted to make a name for himself. There were other items on his goal list also. Max asked me to write a list of goals to be implemented upon arrival to Colorado. There was really only one goal that I could think of and that was "not to commit suicide." But for Max's sake I made up a few more, like getting a good job and being a better girlfriend to Max. I couldn't think of anything else, as I knew in my heart that suicide was going to be my fate wherever I may be living!

Max made some phone calls and sent out his resume to companies in Colorado. He had a friend from the service who was happy to have Max stay with him and his wife while he went for a week to Colorado to secure a job. I drove Max to the Am-Track train station and kissed him goodbye. Max was gone for a full week and I could not stop thinking about the nightmare I had of moving to Colorado. It just seemed like a death trap to move there and never find my way back east.

When the Am-Track arrived bringing Max back to Rhode Island, he seemed like a new man with a strong vision of what he wanted to do in Colorado. I felt like the only thing I would do was to hold him back because of my consistent mental illness.

The day finally came when we were ready to move. I had totaled my car in an accident weeks before, so we just took Max's car and attached it to a large U-Haul. I had just one request and that was to go to Ohio and visit my parents before heading across the country for Colorado. Max agreed, so we first went to Ohio and stayed overnight at my parents' house. I felt so uncomfortable sleeping over that I insisted on Max being fully clothed (as I was) when we went to bed. The next morning, we took off for Colorado. It turned into a five day trip with one or two nights staying at cheap hotels. I behaved horribly all the way to Denver and made Max miserable most of the way. The U-Haul ran out of gas because the gas gauge was off. Max pulled over on the side of the road and unhooked the securely connected car and sent me off to find a gas station, buy a gas can and fill it while he stayed behind with the U-Haul. Not even knowing if I could finish this task, I took off in his car and drove for miles and miles until I found a gas station. When I got back on the freeway I remember having to make an illegal U-turn to get back to where Max was. He filled the U-Haul truck with gas and off we went to find the same gas station where I had gotten the gas.

It seemed like a never ending trip in which Max drove most of the way. He got very angry when I drove and ran over a curb on a city street. The trip across Kansas seemed like weeks instead of hours as the scenery went from field to field to field of farmland.

Looking far in the distance over this completely flat land I saw for the first time, Denver, Colorado. The city seemed huge but all by itself way out there in No Man's Land with this strange cloud of smog looming above it. Beyond it was the beautiful Rocky Mountains, and for the first time I was excited and actually looking forward to the life that Max and I would be starting.

There were many business parks in Denver where all the companies conglomerated into one area. Max had already rented an apartment that was not far from his job. It was a one bedroom in a complex with many other apartments and seemed very small to me. The waterbed was set up first along with the couch and other furniture. We had a small kitchen table in what was called a dining room. The kitchen was just a little hallway, but I was happy to see a dishwasher. Max started work right away while I searched for a job. I actually got two jobs, one at Barbeque Restaurant as a waitress and one at a department store that I had never heard of, simply called "Target." At Target, I worked as a cashier. I also put resumes out for many secretarial positions.

The tension between Max and me became increasingly difficult. Max was working and did not get home until late in the evening. I was filled with loneliness and made a male friend at the apartment complex, a man from another state who was just living in Colorado to finish a construction site. I was lonely and this man was lonely, so I would go over to just talk in the evenings. It was apparent that this man believed that I was a little bit crazy, but he was desperate for someone just to hang out with. I felt my relationship with Max slipping away, but there seemed to be nothing I could do about it.

A phone call came one morning for an interview at an insurance company for a secretary. This job included typing with a headset while listening to insurance claims concerning car accidents and the like. I got the job because of my typing speed which was over 80 words a minute. The woman who made the decision to hire me went out of her way to help me keep my job. She even went as far as giving me rides home from work. I told her that I used to walk on Arapahoe Road to get to and from work at the Restaurant and Target. The woman said "Walking on that road is suicide." I wanted to answer with the word "Precisely!" But I decided not to say it.

In time, it became increasingly hard to go to work and I began calling in sick. My supervisor encouraged me to eat lunch with all the other ladies in order to fit in, but I was still a smoker at the time and would rather just smoke a cigarette instead of eat. There were two 15 minute breaks in an eight hour day and only a half hour for lunch. That was only three breaks for cigarettes. I longed for my job at the bank in Providence where I could smoke freely at my desk with my own ash tray.

I wanted to run away but I had nowhere to go. Everything was going wrong with my relationship with Max, and my supervisor at the insurance company didn't know what to do with me. The depression was slowly overwhelming me and the psychiatrist that I had signed up with did not know what to do with me either. This psychiatrist was a very young woman who may have just gotten out of medical school. She would not answer any of my calls and pleas for help. When I finally got an appointment to see her, it was late in the day and nobody was in the office. I sat in the waiting room and listened as my psychiatrist spoke on the phone to a colleague begging for assistance in this difficult case of a manic-depressive from Rhode Island. When she finally hung up, I went up to the counter, my head hanging low. If the psychiatrist has no confidence in what to do, then how was I supposed to have confidence in her to treat me? Gone were the days of Dr. Radeem who told me I would be okay and that he would take care of me. The conversation between this doctor and myself was very uncomfortable that day with me telling her that I just needed a prescription for lithium.

I was feeling increasingly hopeless. I would take the bus to downtown Denver and walk around the city streets looking for the homeless. I made two goals which were crystal clear. One was to go downtown with my suitcase and live with the homeless people who lived in cardboard boxes, and the other was to eventually commit suicide.

After all, I still held on to that awful nightmare of having a one way trip to Colorado. This meant that I would never get out of the state alive. I tried to commit suicide with an overdose, but then called a friend in Ohio who, in turn, got a hold of the police who broke down the locked apartment door and an ambulance took me to a hospital to get my stomach pumped. During the trip to the hospital, the EMT in the ambulance was so kind to me I will never forget him. He told me that he could not understand why a young girl like me would be trying to commit suicide. He told me that he and his wife had so many bills that they were up to their ears in debt but suicide would never be an option no matter how many problems they had. Listening to his smooth voice comforted me. When we had arrived at the hospital he and another man pulled the gurney out of the ambulance and told me they were thankful I wasn't obese like their last patient. I heard every word they said but could not respond as the drugs were taking effect.

I had had my stomach pumped several times and it was always a horrible experience. Afterward, they gave me liquid charcoal which would neutralize everything in a person's stomach. In Denver, I was awake enough that they insisted that I drink it instead of pumping it into my stomach. It was thick, black and pure charcoal. It tasted horrid but they stayed at my bedside until I swallowed all of it.

Chapter 8

Homeless?

One night in April 1988, Max and I had our final argument. It was the end of our relationship. I packed my suitcase and proceeded to do what I had planned. I left the apartment in the dark and on foot. I walked until I couldn't walk anymore, so I slumped down in a field and put my head on my suitcase for a pillow. I decided that in the morning I would take a bus downtown and begin my new life as a homeless person. I believed that was where I belonged, and truly thought that I would be able to get along with these lost souls, sharing food and alcohol with them and having my own cardboard box. I focused solely on that plan and decided to take the first bus in the morning.

The one thing that I could not help but notice as I looked up at the sparkling sky was the enormity of it. It was beautiful with shimmering stars and a big moon staring down at me. I thought of God and how Jesus had shown his love to me so wonderfully that day in Rhode Island when I was so close to suicide. Where was he now when I was hurting so badly? Could he really be out there somewhere past that illuminated sky? I called for him but he did not answer. Again I thought about how alone I was. No family, no friends, no car, and no hope. The emotional pain of being rejected by Max was eating me up inside, but I knew deep in my heart that it was over between the two of us. I hung out in that field all night thinking about the prospect of living on the streets of Denver and trying to figure out where I would plug in my curling iron and how I would be able to put my make-up on. I needed my "cover" of not looking like a mentally ill person. I thought about the unforgiving brick buildings and the towering skyscrapers downtown. There would be no electric plugs. I also needed my make-up mirror to light up. I had it in my suitcase along with my mascara and other items. It was really not making sense to live on the streets, but I felt that I had nowhere else to live. I refused to go back to Max. I slept a little bit that night and when the sun finally began to rise, it seemed that the morning light gave me a new idea. This would be a last ditch effort to get some help.

In the morning I walked the long trek to the local Mental Health Center, as they were called at that time. I went in and sat in the waiting room not really knowing what to expect. A beautiful African American woman came out and took me aside. I told her of my plan to live on the streets of Denver, and also of my other plan which was to commit suicide. This woman was very strong and convincing, and she insisted that I go live in what they called then "a half-way house," instead of on the streets. I could not get that nightmare out of my mind about the bus driver saying that it was a one way trip to Colorado. It made me certain that I would never leave the state alive, and my plans to live on the streets or commit suicide once and for all were very hard for me to change.

I really didn't want to go to some strange half-way house and live with people I didn't know, especially when I was feeling so screwed up. It took a lot of persuading, but I finally agreed to move into this half-way house that was located in Littleton, Colorado. I walked into the house and right away I told my story to anyone who would listen, again searching, ever searching for one person to be able to help me and my crazy mind. I told everyone that I really didn't see myself living through this period of time in Colorado and didn't want to be in this half-way house at all.

I found that they all shared the same bathroom and shower, and this was a deterrent to me as well, because there were all kinds of different people living there. I couldn't fathom taking a shower where all the others took theirs also. It seemed really gross considering that there was a man living there who really did live on the streets of Denver and he was filthy dirty. The thought of all of them sharing a bathroom really bothered me, but there really wasn't a choice. The only option was that I took on the chore of cleaning the bathroom from top to bottom, and that helped me with the others using it. I also liked to vacuum the entire house upstairs and downstairs. Each week someone different was assigned to cook for everyone, but there was this one man who was an over-the-top fantastic cook. He fried up chicken and made salads that were really amazing, so most of the people living there exchanged chores with him so that he would cook for us every night. Nobody minded cleaning up the kitchen as long as this man did all the cooking.

The gentleman who lived on the streets of Denver fascinated me since I was planning on doing the same thing. I interviewed him about the lifestyle of the homeless. He had a big long fuzzy beard and a weather beaten face. He also didn't have many changes of clothing. He told me how he and others had pulled out their own teeth because they hurt so much and they would have been turned away had they walked into a dentist office. During the winter months they all shared bottles of alcohol which gave them the feeling of being warm for a time, but that it was false warmth that went away very quickly. The winter months were very difficult because the snowfall in that area of the country was monumental. I remembered my first ski trip I went on with Max. We went to his buddy's house and his wife gave me this powder blue all one-piece snow suit to wear. I was thankful because it kept me warm and dry. Max paid for me to take lessons that day, and then finally I had the opportunity to go on the lift and ski down the slope. It was exhilarating and I enjoyed it so much. Max was an avid skier and went down the highest mountain which really was impressive to me since just walking in the boots seemed uncomfortable to me. Max was opening doors to a much broader life than what we had had in Rhode Island.

He seemed so happy living in Colorado; it was just that I had been holding him back with my total dependence on him for the three years we were together.

Emotionally I was a mess at the half-way house because it hurt so bad that we had broken up. Max had always been there when I needed him and he stuck with me a long time considering how badly I hurt HIM at times. He had been the rock I needed during those really difficult times. The pain of the breakup caused even more depression, and I often thought of walking out on the street to get hit by a car. The movie Dirty Dancing had just come out on VHS and they were playing it at the half-way house one evening. I could not watch it because it hurt too much to see the romance in the movie that was so powerful. I cried and cried and cried. There had been a time when Max and I had talked of marriage but soon after Max kind of chickened out and never brought it up again. He did not want to marry a woman who was so emotionally distraught and unsure of every step she took.

The half-way house turned out not to be so bad after all. I had a roommate whose father was a preacher. Anne was a nice girl but seemed to hate the fact that she was brought up in such a strict home. She and I hung out together and talked a lot about what we were going through. We would stay up way past "lights out" and joke around a lot. She had a great sense of humor. One night Anne and I snuck past the sleeping midnight staff person and crept into the room where the staff usually met. Quietly we walked into this forbidden territory to see what the staff was saying about us. On a very large easel was a list with each person's name written in a large red marker, and next to our names was a comment about each of us. I searched out my name and next to it were the words: "Does not take responsibility for her own actions." I took immediate offence at this statement and said to Anne, "But I do take responsibility for my own actions!" Surprisingly, Anne stated, "No you don't." and she gave me a few examples. What an eye-opener. To this day I tell everyone in each class that I teach that Recovery begins with taking responsibility for your own actions – good or bad. This, in turn, has opened up many a discussion over the following years: should or shouldn't a person apologize for their behavior while they were psychotic or depressed? The answer is: YES! Sometimes we say and do things that can really hurt or upset someone else, and we need to own up to our behavior whether *they* remember it or not. It helps us mature. The flip side of this argument is: why do people with other diseases, say diabetes, or heart disease, not see a need to apologize for their illnesses? One reason is that their *behavior* probably is not affected to the extreme as in the case with mental problems. We do not choose our diseases, but we need to be taking responsibility for them. I stand firm on the "responsible for your behavior whether you could help it or not." If we are going to be mental patients, than let's be the *best* mental patients that we can be! That was a great lesson for me to learn.

One day, out of the blue, Max showed up at the half-way house. I was so happy to see him, although he hadn't come to see me but just to drop off a plane ticket that my sister Gini had sent for me to come to Ohio for a visit. I looked at the date for the flight and it was in May, coming up in a few short weeks. It was then that I had a huge burden lifted from me just knowing that I would survive this trip to Colorado and be home in Ohio soon. The excitement lessened when I realized that the plane was to take off at 5:30 AM and I would have to find a person to take me to the Denver Airport. I did not know anyone who would be reliable enough to trust and who owned their own car. In time, I found the right person, but I had to put all of my trust in this girl. If she couldn't take me to the airport that morning, then my entire plan of being set free from this negative place would be lost. I befriended this girl, and the night before my trip, I spent the night with her in a Group Home which was my first experience with permanent housing for the mentally ill. The girl, Sharon, said that she was originally from Boston and that her father ran in the Boston Marathon every year. She was diagnosed with paranoid schizophrenia but was able to drive and took me to the Denver Airport as planned. I asked to get there a bit early so that I could down a few drinks at the airport bar. I had some painkillers in my purse from a trip to the dentist, so I swallowed a handful of them and then quickly drank as many drinks as I had time for at the bar, spending every last dime I had on alcohol. Needless to say, I was not just manic, but drunk and high on painkillers for this long flight across the country. There were no stops or layovers. It was a one way trip to Ohio!

I sat down in the airplane wearing a cowboy hat and cowboy boots and feeling like an out-of-control caged animal. The seat was too small and I was squished up next to a young couple in the aisle seat. At first the couple sitting next to me made some small talk, but soon had that "look" in their eyes of fear and concern. Before the plane took off, the lighted signs and stewardesses told everyone to put on their seatbelts. When I refused, they asked me a couple more times and even had a male steward come and try to persuade me. Even when driving in a car, I refused to wear a seatbelt because if there was an accident, I wanted to make sure that I had a better chance of dying. At this point the stewardess gave up. I kept screaming at them to bring me a stiff drink, which they all refused to do. I decided that if I wasn't going to be given any alcohol, then I wasn't going to sit in my assigned seat either! "Screw this!" I yelled and leaped out of my seat and ran to the back of the airplane. Once there, I laid down flat on the floor of the airplane, and enjoyed the loud vibration and noise of the engine. I was lying between the two restrooms and when anyone would come back to use the restroom, I would point with my cowboy boot to the right or the left, depending if they were male or female. I kept on yelling at first, but when a man from the front of the plane calmly told me that I must keep very quiet, I listened to him. But even after much persuasion, I would not leave my place lying on the floor in the back of the plane.

Chapter 9

The Homecoming

The year was 1988. I figure that if this had happened in 2013, the airplane may have landed and let me off because the other people on the plane were quite scared and/or annoyed at this "crazy girl's" behavior. When the plane finally landed at the Cleveland Airport, I skipped off the plane and ran into my sister Gini's arms. "Oh, Gin, it is so good to see you!" I climbed into her bright red Mustang convertible and we zoomed out of the airport parking lot on our way to the Ohio Turnpike. At first the plan was to have me stay with Gini and her husband in Port Clinton, Ohio, but by the short time we had made it to the turnpike, Gini was adamant that I stay at our parents' house. It was obvious to her that she was not going to be able to handle her sister, and in fact, she was a little afraid of me. When we pulled into the driveway of my parents' house in Cortland, Ohio, I sat in fear of being rejected by my father. I had already put them through so much over the years. But as we climbed out of the car, our mother and father, Joan and Stew McCurdy came out of the house and down the steps to greet us. My father said "Welcome home!" It was a wonderful moment for me. I was finally walking on Ohio ground and looking at my parents, so thankful to be alive and safe at my childhood home.

I began looking for a job and while scouring the newspaper I saw an ad for a "Singing Telegram" company located in Akron, Ohio.

It didn't take me long to interview for and begin learning telegram songs and jokes. They asked me which type of telegrams I would be interested in. All in all I have dressed up in a Chicken Suit, a Tuxedo, a Genie from the Bottle outfit, Mae West (which paid the most) and A Bag Lady. I was told to have paper and pencil ready every time the phone rang so that I could quickly jot down all of the details for the singing telegram. I also was given a very large helium tank that I kept in my parent's basement along with many Mylar balloons because each telegram included ten balloons that I had to blow up.

I really enjoyed doing the telegrams because it didn't matter if I was manic or depressed or in between, I had the songs and the acts and jokes memorized so I could do a telegram at the drop of a hat. The telegrams were very sensual in nature, especially the Genie and Mae West. For Mae West I wore a $300.00 dress that the company provided, and I would put socks in the breast area to be a little more realistic to the character. I performed these telegrams for almost two years in all capacities and places from busy restaurants to large corporations to people's homes to outdoor bonfires, and one time at a wedding reception. The people who worked for the company wrote the songs and the jokes and everything was all laid out for us. Once in a while I would have two telegrams in one night, so I would bring my other costume and change in the restroom of a gas station or somewhere, going into the bathroom dressed as a chicken and coming out dressed as a Genie from the bottle. My supervisors were trying desperately to talk me into being a playboy bunny, but I didn't think I had the body for it. Just before I left the company, they had come up with a Marilyn Monroe act that they wanted me to try out. I said no to that one too.

During this tenure of working for the singing telegram company, I fell into a deep depression. I had called Dr. Radeem who insisted that I go into the psychiatric ward at St. Joseph's Riverside Hospital. I called the agency and told them that I was suffering from Hepatitis, not knowing anything about the illness. The first question I was asked was, "Which one-- A, B or C?" I just guessed and chose "B".

I didn't care what they thought, just as long as they didn't know that I was in depression.

While I was in the hospital I was allowed to go home on a pass. When I arrived back in the psych ward I was wearing my chicken suit dressed as "Chadwick Chicken" carrying my little son named "Egg-Bert" The nurses were aware that it was me and got all the patients together so that I could do my routine for them. The song was to the tune of "I am Woman Hear me Roar" and went something like this:

"I am chicken hear me roar, "Bawk"
Don't mistake me for a duck "Quack"
And I know today's a very special day!
I flew in from my roost, just to give your day a boost,
'cause you're special in each and every way.
Oh yes! I am here, 'cause your friends think you are dear,
They tell me, you're egg septional.
I am strong! I am impeccable! I am chicken!"

The chicken singing telegram was the only one that could be done for children as all the others were for "mature audiences." The folks in the psych ward enjoyed the show, and I thought it was so funny that they did not know who I was until I took the head of the chicken off.

Although I had explicit directions from the singing telegram people not to wear the head of the chicken while driving, (there were very small eye holes and no peripheral vision) one day I was stopped at a busy intersection at a very long red light. I thought about it for a moment and then put the top of the chicken on as I already had the suit on. When the light turned red for the cars going north and south, a semi- traffic jam started as all eyes were on this little Chevy Chevette with a chicken driving. I thought it was absolutely hilarious and had a great laugh, but just to be on the safe side, I never again put the head on while driving.

When I came out of the hospital I had lost 15 pounds which made me slimmer than ever. I had been told that Prozac makes a person lose weight, and so, being on Prozac for the first time, I subconsciously believed that I would lose weight, and I did. One of the nurses who had known me for years commented, "Most patients taking psychotropic drugs gain a large amount of weight, but you never did. You look great!" This made me feel great as I was constantly trying to let others know that you don't have to gain weight on these medications.

The men at the singing telegram company wanted me to learn the Playboy Bunny routine now that I had lost weight. I still refused because I did not think I would look good enough. I was very aware that men (actually more so women for that matter) scrutinize your body when you are acting the part during a singing telegram. Although I never had anyone say anything negative about my looks, I lacked the confidence I knew my "trouble spots." With this in mind, I was doing an outdoor party dressed as Mae West. I got paid the most when I did the Mae West act because it called for me to bring background music and sing with a dance routine. Also, it was extravagant and extremely sexual. The lines were actually the same as what Mae West said in her movies, *if ya know what I mean!* I had the lines down so well that I forgot that evening just what could happen when men were drunk. One of the men would not leave me alone. He was so drunk that he was staggering around and acting pretty much like an idiot. When I was done performing, this man asked me "How much would you charge to show me your **"socks"**? (Not the word he used.) He said "I will give you $40.00!" I thought for a moment. *If* I bent over and showed him my thick yellow and pink socks what would this man do? Say I was a fraud?   Many things ran through my mind when the light bulb went off! This man will see my yellow and pink socks but would feel like really stupid in front of his friends if he just spent $40.00 for a 'look' at a pair of socks. I decided to go for it thinking this would be the biggest tip I ever got. I took the $40.00 and then bent down and showed this fella my socks. I figured right!   He ran off bragging to his buddies about what he saw while I quickly grabbed my belongings and took off. I got the last laugh that night! Most of the jokes were kind of making fun of the person who the singing telegram was for.

One night I was called to do a Genie-from-the Bottle singing telegram for a Youngstown restaurant owner. I was in a deep depression and really just wanted to get it over with as quickly and painlessly as possible. I went through all the motions and said all the nasty jokes, sang the song and wanted to bolt out of there. To make matters worse this man's family were standing around him like a protective shield and they did not laugh at any of the jokes on cue, nor did they seem very happy with the telegram, to say the least. I could feel the tension around me mounting through one dirty joke after the other. I could not wait to leave! As soon as I turned toward the door, the wife of the restaurant owner came out and told me off. She was very angry and I was so filled with such despair I couldn't even argue back. I wanted to explain to her that I did not write the material and if she wanted the telegram to be "clean" she should have told the agency when she called. She started ranting at me, "How dare you make fun of my husband! He has owned and operated this restaurant for years and deserves respect, not nasty jokes! We did not appreciate you degrading a very well-respected man in this community!" And then it happened. The absolute worst thing that I was always so afraid may happen; this woman could actually see my depression through my smile! She said "And you, you are not even happy. I can tell by your eyes that you are not happy. You shouldn't be doing these singing telegrams, they are raunchy and you are so unhappy you actually look deeply depressed!" That did it. Adios, Amigo! I ran to my car holding back the tears. I drove home crying and contemplating suicide over and over in my mind.

The next morning, the call came through from the singing telegram company. "Don't worry about it, Nancy, we get a lot of complaints and most of them are not because of your act. You did what we taught you to do, so don't take it personally." It was apparent that this woman had called and complained. I felt horrible.

Once in a while when the phone rang and my supervisor gave me directions he would say "Now, Nancy, you must make this one clean. No dirty jokes at all." I would think "Oh brother, it's those Christians again! They don't like the dirty jokes!" These particular telegrams were extremely hard to do as each time I would look at my joke list and pull out the clean ones to memorize. I had my own ideas about Christians…they were what I called "squeaky clean" and judgmental. They would try to talk you into believing in Jesus and then walk away as though you were too dirty a person to truly be friends with. I knew some Christians and I really did not like them. The one interesting thing that I did notice was when I swore and said "Jesus Christ," a strange peace would come over me. In fact, because of this, I said "Jesus!" a lot. It was very noticeable, and it would not be long until I would be surrounded by Christians who prayed very hard for my conversion.

Hospitalizations

I was hospitalized many times again at St. Joe's and made several friends that I had later wished I hadn't. Sometimes it was really difficult to get along with people while in the ward, depending on what illnesses they had. We all used to sit in a big circle and smoke cigarettes and talk. One woman, Connie, had a manicure kit which I used and gave everyone manicures and painting all of their fingernails pink, the only color that I had. Once in a while there would be someone really nasty and mean who would tell me off. One girl named Klarissa scared the pants off of me when she got straight into my face and yelled at me for a good five minutes. She told me that she was going to kill me when we got out of there. After meeting with my psychiatrist the next morning and telling him what happened, he told me not to worry. He was told the same thing by her.

Some days when things were really getting rowdy with all the arguing I would stand up and said "Hey, come on, listen to yourselves! You would think we were all mentally ill or something!" This would break the icy frowns into a smirk, at least for the moment. Or I may stand up and say something like "Listen, we are all a little bit off our rockers right now or we would not be in here, so let's give each other a break!"

During my numerous hospitalizations at St. Joe's, there were certain protocols that I was just plain getting tired of. One of which was continual urine tests. I got so sick of handing in urine samples that when asked one morning for "yet another" urine specimen, I quietly poured Diet Coke into the cup and added water until I believed it would pass for slightly dark urine. It was then sent to the lab, tested, and the results were added to my thick file. At the time I didn't understand nor did it even dawn on me that the staff was checking for street drugs. As a week or so went by and I did not hear anything about this Diet Coke urine specimen and I decided to "come clean" and ask a nurse about it. The lab result was looked up in my file. The nurse read it over and then showed it to me. To my surprise, the urine test came out just fine except for an elevated content of caffeine. I was even more surprised when later two other nurses approached me with concern as to why I played this "trick." I told the truth, I was sick and tired of urine tests as I was also subconsciously sick and tired of staying in and out of "Mental Hotels." The psychiatrist was notified and he, too, looked at me with concern. I said "Come on, doctor, all of this is getting really old!" I couldn't to this day even count how many times I was hospitalized for depression.

It got SO bad, these long visits of searching for stability that I decided to REALLY do something bad. I had taken a test called an MMPI which stands for Minnesota Multiphasic Personality Inventory probably seven or eight times in my life. It is LONG! It has 400 true/false questions! It takes over an hour to complete and, to be honest; I just plain did not want to answer these questions again when the test was administered to me the last time I was in St. Joe's. The questions repeat themselves over and over written in different ways and after taking it so many times and always answering truthfully, I decided enough was enough. If the psychologists didn't know me by now, well, I would show them a "new side of Nancy" they had never seen before. I sat down and began answering the questions. I decided to lie on the test and see what would happen. Boy, did I find out!!! After handing it in I was almost immediately called in for a meeting. When I walked into the meeting room I nearly turned around and walked back out. It was Mr. LaLome!!! The therapist I had when I was 17 years old! "Oh Boy!" I thought. Years had passed and he looked older…and wiser! He was now working in forensics and had some questions for me about the test. I sat down across from him and said "We meet again." He said, "Yes, Nancy." very professionally. "I have some concerns about your MMPI test, Nancy."

"Oh, okay, what is the problem?" I asked nervously.

He answered that this test did not line up with all of the other MMPI's I had taken and that I never before answered the questions this way.

"Do you hear voices that tell you to kill someone?" he asked.

I said "Of course not!"

"Have you ever physically hurt a pet?"

"No." I sheepishly answered.

Then I decided to tell him the truth before I was in deeper water. "Mr. LaLome, you remember me from years ago, right?" He nodded. "So you see how long I've been dealing with this MMPI test. I just wanted to see what would happen if I answered a few "true" that should have been answered "false", and, well, now I found out!"

That was the last time I was given an MMPI test and the last time I saw Mr. LaLome. What a relief!

Soon after the singing telegram stint, I got a temporary secretary position at the local car assembly plant again. This was where I came across Christians who made friends with me and explained how they felt and lived while believing in Jesus. I was interested when another secretary told me that she was in charge of the supply cabinet in my department. I asked Debbie if she ever stole anything from the cabinet which was right behind her desk, and since she kept the inventory, nobody would know. Debbie explained to me that at one point in her life she probably would have stolen from the supply cabinet, but since she had put her faith in God, she would never steal because she knew it was wrong. I pondered this over many times, thinking Debbie was a pretty cool lady. There was also a man who was employed there whose son was in my graduating class and I had known him for years. He was very friendly and also very godly. He spoke to me a lot and encouraged me by telling me about a God who loved me for who I was and would never judge me.

While this was going on, I was befriending many people in the offices and plant of Warren Assembly. I was still a smoker so I would have to go out into the plant to have a cigarette, leaving my office desk for long periods of time. The word had gotten out that I had done singing telegrams and I was asked if I would be willing to jump out of a cake in a bikini for somebody's birthday at the plant. I was flattered but quietly declined. While out in the plant, I had a lot of good times talking to people, especially a gentleman by the name of Tony. Tony was extremely handsome and his wife had passed away, so he was definitely available. I spent a lot of time with Tony, going out to lunch and spending time at bars with him. He would meet my friend Chrissy and me at certain bars for Karaoke. He also had a jet ski and would take me out on it during the summer months. But there was something deep seated wrong with Tony, as if he were walking around in a bit of a fog, and his memory was really bad. One night I was at his house watching a movie, and the next day at work he started to tell me about this great movie he saw on TV the night before. I said "Tony, I was with you!" He was a bit embarrassed. I never asked him any questions about his wife at all, being afraid to bring it up. Whenever I was with Tony I would act manic and all bubbly, always hiding my depression from him. Once he asked me to come to his house for dinner. While there I was falling deep into a depression and so I layed on his couch until it was time to eat. He was an excellent cook and I ate with him and his two children forcing myself all the while to pretend to be happy.

One evening while we sat at one of the local bars, Tony revealed to Chrissy that his wife had actually committed suicide. What a shock! I was jealous that he didn't feel comfortable enough to tell me himself. I couldn't figure out why he confided in Chrissy. Needless to say, when I found out about it I was devastated for him and his two children. I got a really bad feeling inside about it, knowing that I, too, was a person who was a candidate for suicide—but she really did it! Oh! Poor Tony! It explained why he was so foggy. Not long after, I blurted out to him that I was involved with a group called "The Manic-Depressive Support Group." Although he never showed much emotion, he kept asking why I wanted to be a part of a support group like that. I told him, "just to help the people who suffer from it" as if it had nothing to do with my own problems.

At this time, I was living in a beautiful remodeled apartment which was very clean and comfortable. I liked living on my own. My friend Chrissy and I would go out every Wednesday and Friday to a place called Sir Bentleys and sing karaoke. Chrissy was my biggest fan and would always give me the thumbs up when I sang. Depending on who all was there, we would depend on men to buy us drinks and both of us smoked heavily. Many times I would come stumbling into my apartment late at night with the room reeling. I was doing what I always did with men. Dated one and had two on hand "just in case" the other wouldn't work out. I was dating a man named Joshua, the man at the plant named Tony, and another gentleman who had the worst OCD (obsessive compulsive disorder) I had ever seen.

During this time period the only meal I would eat was lunch, and boy, did the folks working at Warren Assembly like to go to good restaurants during lunch, often going over the allotted time of one full hour just to eat. I loved my boss and felt very comfortable working there. But I did tell lies and played games with people. In fact, all my life I wounded men's egos because "hurting people, hurt people." I liked to play a game of really caring about a man, and then all at once turn my back on him, not answering calls and not allowing him to see me. It felt good for me to hurt them because emotionally I was unable to feel any empathy. I was still experiencing mood swings and the pain never ended.

I had been encouraged by some of the women from Warren Assembly to try out for a play called "Transparencies" that the local Ladies of Musical Art was hosting. It was to be held at Woodview Auditorium. I not only tried out for this play, but I got a lead part! I had a solo to memorize and a duet and many lines. In the play my name was Bonnie Bean, part of the Bean family. There were many women from the group who were not happy that I got a lead part because they wanted the part to go to someone who was part of the Ladies Group. I remember the solo very well; it was called "On My Own" from the play *Les Miserables*, and the duet was with the character named Benny in the play called "Walk through the World with Me." The man who played the part of Benny was 40 years old, worked at Sharon Steel, and lived across the border in Pennsylvania. I remember thinking he was old, being 40, but he certainly didn't look old or act old. Age is really just a number, and I believe I was around 28 at the time.

The play was a great success and we did two performances in front of a full house at Woodview Auditorium But wait, I do recall a bit of drama. We had to practice many evenings and at one practice close to the opening of the show, I was feeling terribly depressed. The woman who played my mother and the man who played my father and I believe my stage brother as well, were treating me like garbage in real life. When it was our cue to go up and prepare to enter the stage, I lagged behind. While the director was looking for me, I was muttering to myself that I just wanted to end it all, and that nasty woman who played my mother had better watch out because I have a mental disorder and her treating me badly did not help. At that point I did not care if I was alive or not—let alone in the play. After that night, the director had us all huddle up on the stage and he explained how he chose each person for the different parts of the play. I was sitting there on the stage with everyone else, but feeling very low. The director took a look at me and said, "And I chose Nancy because she is beautiful and can sing." Well, that was like music to my ears; but then, some of the women disliked me even more. Oh! If only they knew the hell I had lived through on this earth.

One afternoon I was feeling quite manic at work when I got a "brilliant" idea. I would borrow someone's radio and take it to the entrance of the building when nobody was around, and then call the radio station and ask if I could sing a song on the radio. Most of the folks in the plant had the same radio station on loud and clear, so it was very exciting for me to sing for everyone in the plant. I called the radio station and the DJ got my name and he actually allowed me to sing. I sang a Linda Ronstadt song as loud and clear as I could, live and in person over the radio. By this time my boss was looking for me, and someone from the department spotted me singing at the entrance of the building. My boss plus a few others came out to see what I was doing. I didn't care who saw me or that it was really time to get work done—if I wanted to sing on the radio, then by darned, I would!

During the time I worked at this temporary job, Debbie and Marcus, (the father of one of my school classmates) kept talking to me about this Jesus person. At Christmas I was asked by Debbie what I wanted for Christmas. I replied, with a grin, "Just a good looking, well-built man who can't talk." I waited for her to give me a lecture about how "bad" I was, but instead of chastising me, Debbie made a very creative booklet for me for Christmas that had pictures of a good looking man from a magazine. I loved it and thought "Wow, this Christian woman is cool."

I was feeling some pressure at this point, like a sudden knowledge that was really affecting the way I thought about good and evil, right from wrong. It was not a good feeling, it was as though I knew that there was a change that was going to happen on the inside of me, and I was in for a ride. I always tell the story of how "someone invited me to church" on December 15, 1991, but it

90

wasn't a person on the earth who invited me; it was truly God himself.

I was lying in bed on the eve of December 15, 1991 trying to fall asleep. I felt the need to pray, although I did not know who I was praying to really, or even how to pray. I began asking God why I was feeling like getting slobbering drunk was wrong. I felt there was nothing wrong with it, but I was getting a sickening feeling about it… like it just wasn't what I should be doing. Also, I was asking him why I suddenly felt it was wrong to have sex outside of marriage. Now that's a crazy thought! Again, I could not see what was wrong with it but was very curious to know why I was changing my mind on these things. I wanted to know why I felt it was important for me to attend a church all of a sudden. I finally slipped into dreamland and slept peacefully for many hours. Suddenly I awoke frightened. I had felt someone blow into my left ear very strongly. This was not just a blowing *into* my ear, but at the same time blowing *out of* my ear. It was powerful. But just as powerful were the words I heard audibly, "To get into heaven." When this happened, I leapt out of bed looking around to see if anyone was there actually speaking to me. The clock said 5:00 AM. I thought long and hard about this experience I just had. "What? Are you kidding me? To get into heaven, what did that mean? Why would it be so important to get into heaven?" I asked myself. But I felt this pulling on my heart and just knew that something had to be done about it.

My psychiatrist did not deem me to be manic as of late, nor depressed; in fact I had been feeling pretty normal for a time. I realized it was a Sunday morning, and although I had heard of North-Mar church because that was where Marcus attended, I really didn't know where it was located or how to get there from my apartment. I did know where the Baptist Church was because my friend Chrissy lived right next door to it for a time, so I got dressed in the morning, not even knowing what time the service started. But honestly, there was no questioning it. I just *had* to go to a church that morning!

Chapter 10

My Conversion to Christianity

I was wearing my sexiest dress and my highest heels as I strutted into this old Baptist church. I was very surprised to see that there was just this large choir singing beautiful songs about Christ being born on Christmas Day, and the words were so touching that I found myself wanting to cry. I sat there in a pew, and realized that I could not EVEN TAKE another breath if I didn't respond to this choir singing words about Christ and his birthday. It was true then. Christ was born in a lowly manger and died on a cross to save people so that they can go to heaven when they die. I recalled the day in Rhode Island when I felt the love of Jesus like a blanket over my body. After the concert, there was given what is called an "altar call." I was sitting there stiff, feeling paralyzed, afraid to go up in front of all these church members and ask for this Jesus to come into my life because it seemed so embarrassing. I could sing in front of a bar but was suddenly afraid to be in front of this group. There was a song playing and people singing "Just as I Am" and I thought... just as I am? Is that how God takes you? I really felt the desire to go up front as the preacher kept asking: if a person wants to get saved, come on up front. Finally, when it was almost over, I went up to the front of the church. The pastor had a look on his face like, "This thing is never going to end; now this young woman is up here wanting salvation." The pastor's wife, whom I found out, was named Lynette, came and spoke with me, and I repeated the words knowing that this was IT; this was the biggest decision I had ever made in my life. Afterward I saw a friend and her husband with whom I'd gone to high school with. She had been a majorette. She now looked at me and said "Welcome to the family." I was not sure what she meant at the time, but thought it was very nice of her to say that.

From that day forward, things began to change for me. I bought a Bible that very same day at Sam's Club, a Rainbow King James Version. I was getting new tires on my car and my parents were there with me. My mother kept telling me that I didn't want the King James Bible and that I should purchase one that is easier to read, like the NIV Bible, but I was adamant about buying the King James Version. I overheard my parents talking, and my mother said, "Well, if all she wants is a Bible, then how bad could that be?" I couldn't wait to get that Bible home so that I could begin reading it and seeing what God had to say about me, and especially what God had to say about manic-depression.

The first thing I wanted to do was to join that beautiful group of men and women singing in that choir—the choir that had drawn me into a full realization of who Christ was and how important it was to invite Him into my life forever. I began attending the Baptist church weekly and going to choir practice to sing in the choir each Sunday morning. I listened intently to each sermon and began seeing changes happening in my life. The first and foremost change that I noticed was a need to pray every night when I went to bed. I had no idea how to pray or what to say, so I prayed silently to myself. Then God put a prayer into my heart. It was to quit smoking. Now I had no intention of quitting smoking at this point. I had smoked for 12 years and had a two and a half pack-a day-habit. The interesting thing was that I did not think of asking to quit smoking, it was the Lord himself nudging me to pray to quit smoking. I just did what I felt I had to do. One night as I was praying, I felt the habit of smoking beginning to leave me, but I panicked and thought, "Oh, no, I'm not ready yet!" Right then the smoking habit came back to me. It was so amazing, so supernatural, I really didn't understand it.

I was still dating a man named Joshua during this time of my new life. We had actually met the first week I was back from Colorado. Joshua was very persistent with me, always wanting to get together, and he had asked me to marry him several times in the short time that I had known him. I knew I couldn't or shouldn't marry Joshua as we just were not compatible, although he was good looking and could be quite a nice guy. One night, on August 24, 1992, I was lying in bed and ready to go to sleep, when I began praying fervently about quitting smoking.

Before I let you know what happened that night; I need to fill you in on what was happening up until that time when it came to my cigarettes. Since I was praying to quit, I noticed that I would be smoking a cigarette and then forget about it and accidently leave it to smolder in the ashtray. I would discover the burnt up cigarette and then light another one, getting very angry. The other thing that kept happening was — I would lose my pack of smokes. I would go buy a pack and then they would disappear. It was getting frustrating!

My sister Linda called one day from Maryland and asked if Joshua and his son Joseph and I would like to come for a weekend visit. Linda told me that she wanted me to sing a solo at her church since I had already sung two solos at the Baptist church. I said "Sure!" And we packed up and drove the six hours to Maryland. Prior to this, I decided I would do something to ensure that I would not run out of cigarettes on this trip. I went out and bought an entire carton, something that I hadn't done before except during the long hospital stays. That Sunday morning, while in Maryland, I made sure I had my cigarettes as I thought there was no way I would be able to go in front of the church and sing a solo without my cigarettes to keep me calm. Linda and I got up early and went to the church

94

where I was to practice the hymn "Because He Lives" with the church pianist. After we practiced the song a few times, I went outside with my purse and opened it up only to find that *I had no cigarettes*. "This *is not funny, God! I NEED a cigarette right now!*" I asked Linda, a former smoker herself, to please go buy me a pack of Benson and Hedges Menthol. For those of you reading this that smoke or have smoked, you know that you have a favorite brand and no other type of cigarette can take its place. Linda went to the store and when she came back she had a pack of Benson and Hedges Menthol Lights. "Linda, these are Lights!" I exclaimed. Oh well. I jumped in her car and drove away from the church down a little dirt road. I was very angry because I wanted *my* cigarettes, not these Lights. I knew how much time I had until the service started, and so I lit one cigarette after another and sucked in as much of the smoke as I possibly could. Then I drove back to the church. At the church I sang my solo with no problem, and afterwards the three of us packed back up and we headed back to Ohio after having a fun-filled trip to Maryland.

Okay, now back to the night of the miracle.

I was praying to quit smoking when in an instant, I felt the poison of the cigarettes showing up in each and every cell of my body. Most people that I knew spoke of lung cancer being the result of smoking, but I had this newfound knowledge that it was poisonous to an entire body, from the top of the head to the bottom of the feet. I suddenly felt the need for some fresh air. I sat up and slowly walked over to the nearest open window. I took a deep breath and exhaled. I took another deep breath and exhaled slowly. The fresh outdoor air never felt so good! I had not taken such a deep breath in years as my lungs were filled with smoke. I had also suffered from many bouts with bronchitis, coughing and coughing, and having trouble breathing. I felt the cigarette habit leave my body completely. Later I was informed that this was called being "delivered" from an addiction by the Lord.

In the morning light, I woke up and felt good, but I started to doubt what had happened the night before. After all, I was a manic depressive, and could this all have been some kind of delusion? My fears were soon abated as Joshua woke up. He looked at me with the strangest look on his face and kept stating that he had had a dream. This was something totally foreign as Joshua had never told me his dreams before, or that he even had them. He sat up and spoke, "Nancy, I had this amazing dream about you and I don't know how to take it. You and I were playing cards just like we were last night. You got two cards that matched and were extremely excited because, of course, that meant that you won the game! You looked at these two matching cards with a big smile on your face that quickly turned to horror. One of the cards had a picture of your cigarettes, Benson and Hedges Menthol; the other card was a picture of you in a coffin with a big cross on it. It was like a cartoon because it had little bubbles as though you were speaking and you were saying 'I am dying for a cigarette.' " I was shocked as Joshua drew these two cards on two large yellow sticky pads. I leaped out of bed and said I was never going to smoke again. I went through everything and threw all of my cigarettes in the garbage. I did not gain a single pound nor have I craved a cigarette since. That was 20 years ago.

Joshua and his son Joseph began attending the Baptist church together with me. Joseph was quite an adorable little boy, but each time his high energy level kept him squirming in his seat, I felt bad for him. Joshua went up to the altar one Sunday and gave his life to the Lord. I was very happy about this and believed that Joshua could quit drinking as I had quit smoking. When Joshua drank he got very mean and acted like a different person. He didn't get drunk that often, but when he did, he was not someone I wanted to be around.

After I had quit smoking, the pastor at the Baptist Church asked me if I would like a job as the secretary to the school principal. I was very excited and told him I would love to take the job. At the same time that I was hired, Joshua and I were called in for a meeting with Pastor Miller and his wife, Lynette. They were very concerned because they believed that Joshua and I may be living together. I explained that I was living with my parents in Cortland at the time and Joshua was living in a duplex in Warren. The Pastor began asking some personal questions about whether we were having sex. We answered as truthfully as we knew how at the time. As Joshua and I nervously laughed, the pastor said "That settles it! You two are to be married as soon as possible. How about this Saturday?" I was shocked and, unfortunately, at the time did not know the difference between the leading of God and the influence of man, especially a man of God. As we walked out of the church that day, Joshua was rejoicing, but I was not rejoicing because I was to have this quick-shotgun wedding without my family there. My three sisters were very upset that they weren't invited. I did invite my sister Chris, only to take pictures. The only people who were at the wedding were my parents, Joshua's parents and Joshua's children, Kerry Ann and Joseph. Kerry Ann, a beautiful young girl who looked a lot like her father, walked down the aisle as the bridesmaid, and Joseph was the best man. Pastor Miller led the ceremony as his wife Lynette sat and watched, along with a man from the church named Mr. White who sat in the back pew. Mr. White had insisted on coming to "pray" throughout the service. I had my hair done and hated it. I also did not like the white suit that I had purchased as a wedding gown. The only things that were beautiful were the flowers and the weather. It was a gorgeous fall day.

Pastor Miller and his wife Lynette were adamant that Joshua and I could not go on a honeymoon since I was not allowed to take any time off from work. There were so many strict rules that I had a hard time figuring it all out. Okay, I was not allowed to wear pants, not allowed to wear any blouses that would show cleavage of any sort, and basically a turtle neck everyday seemed to be what they were looking for. I realized soon enough that all of my short dresses had to go and be replaced by long ones below the knee. The one thing I refused to conform to was the shoes. I wore my high spiked heels even though Lynette Miller told me I needed to buy some flats. I tried to follow the rules. There seemed to be many rules and it was a very strict school. Even stricter was the fact that I had to go to church every Sunday and never miss a Wednesday night service. In the Baptist "culture" missing a Wednesday night meant you were "backsliding." The school also did not have much money and I had to bring in my own typewriter to use to type up files. One of my jobs was to give out "demerits" to children who misbehaved. I wanted to be lenient to these poor little kids who were forced to dress a certain way and forced to be good as gold, but the principal made the rules. After collecting so many demerits, the children would then be called into the principal's office for a "talk". There also was talk of Pastor Miller and Lynette retiring and giving the pastoral responsibility to a young married couple. When that happened, disaster struck the church and the school, but I stayed out of it.

Believing Baptist

I used to go into the gym to eat my lunch with the teachers and it was not long until I noticed that I was being ostracized—for what, I did not know. Because I felt uncomfortable eating lunch with all these women who mostly wore no make-up and wore the most boring clothes I had ever seen, I decided to eat my lunch at my desk. One day, the principal called me into his office. I was concerned that I would now be in trouble just like a child. I went in and sat down. He asked me why I didn't eat my lunch with the rest of the school staff. I explained that I felt very uncomfortable with the women as they did not seem to want to socialize with me in any way. The principal turned his head and said, "It is because you are drop dead gorgeous!" I looked at him in shock! Wow! This was my first experience with a man of God acting out of character. I excused myself and went back to my office which was adjacent to the principal's office. Each and every time I was introduced to another teacher or faculty member, whoever was introducing me would always end up saying "Nancy just recently got saved." Okay, was that an excuse for why I was wearing high heels?

My marriage to Joshua was also on shaky ground. Although, we were not allowed to go on a honeymoon, Joshua and I did go to a hotel room for one night. It was an obvious night of seeing into the future like a "looking glass" as I lie there trying to sleep while Joshua had a football game on the TV blaring loudly. Joshua had what seemed to be an addiction to watching sports whereas I had no interest whatsoever. I soon learned the cliché "Football Widow" and that is what I called myself during our short marriage.

I was feeling like everyone wanted to control me, from the Baptist school to my husband, and also there was the stress of taking care of young Joseph. I was beginning to get very anxious. The kicker was when December came along and I was told that although the children had a Christmas vacation, I, as an employee, was to work every day except for Christmas itself. This really upset me. I had had two weeks off in a row while working at Warren Assembly, and what kind of work was there to do while the children were not in the building? I had made plans to go visit my sister Gini in Port Clinton during my time off. When I explained this to the pastors, they made me sign a slip to have a few days off. I went to visit my sister and had a good time, but was feeling very anxious and unable to sleep.

When I got back to Warren, I made the decision to go into the psychiatric hospital. After all, is this not the only escape from real life that I had learned? I was very anxious at the time. While in the psychiatric ward, I was told that I had some visitors. It was the principal and the new pastor –to- be and his wife. They did not know what to say to me and had no idea that I had ever suffered from depression. It was a very awkward prayer when the four of them held hands and the pastor kept repeating, "Lord, we do not understand this." As they prayed for me and my "mind," I was wishing that they hadn't made the effort to come and see me. It was obvious that this church and psychiatric problems did not mix.

What I didn't know was that there was a big world out there of different denominations that were not legalistic about clothing and shoes. I learned a lot from working at the Baptist school, but it wasn't until I moved on to another church and joined women in Bible studies and read the Bible myself every day that I truly learned the power of the Lord and the power of prayer. I must admit though that God knew what He was doing in my life when I walked into the Baptist church for the first time. I needed to learn about modesty.

99

I was asked by my psychiatrist to go to an outpatient program while I was married to Joshua. Each morning at 8:00 AM a van would pull into my driveway and I would be taken to the outpatient location. I absolutely loved going there every day. I made friends with the nurses and the patients and even began curling all the ladies' hair with my new hair curler. It was one of those "seen on TV" special curlers and I wanted to help them all look beautiful and feel beautiful. Early on, I was told by one of the nurses that I wasn't allowed to sing because it echoed throughout the building and bothered her. This was very disappointing to me as one of my ways of making myself feel better was to sing wherever I was. My psychiatrist stopped in each day to speak to me and I enjoyed this outpatient facility immensely. It was run by a man named Tommy who was himself a runner. He would jog into the building every morning in his shorts. I thought he was nice and he really seemed to care about the patients there. The only time of the day that I disliked was when the van took me home in the afternoon.

Every time we had an argument, Joshua would point to the front door and say "There's the door!" I did not have a key to the house for some reason, so every so often I would come home to an empty locked house. I would have to go to the neighbors and borrow their ladder. I would put the ladder up to the kitchen window above the kitchen sink, open it, and crawl into that small window head first trying not to hit the faucet and get wet. I would then unlock the door and go outside to return the ladder. I often wondered if Joshua was locking me out on purpose. Walking out the front door, as Joshua repeatedly suggested, began to look very appealing to me.

Chapter 11

Believing For a Miracle turned into Disaster

My friend Chrissy introduced us to a new church and Joshua and I started attending there. This church was very different from the Baptist church, and I liked the freedom of wearing whatever you wanted—yes, even blue jeans! Chrissy and I became very close again, but this time our focus was on church and the Bible instead of bars and men. I was also working at General Electric every other day through a temporary agency. I really enjoyed my job and it was nice that some weeks I only worked Tuesdays and Thursdays while other weeks I worked Monday, Wednesday, and Friday. The woman who trained me was also a Christian and she was very intelligent and helpful. At this church, which was called "Foursquare" I was introduced to praying in the Spirit or, in other words, speaking in tongues. It is a very powerful gift from the Lord but at first I was not comfortable practicing it. It was all so new to me. I sang a few solos at this church with background CD's. When I shook because of my Lithium medication, the pastor said he just thought I was engaged in the Spirit so strongly that it made me quiver all over. Joshua was always very encouraging and often told me that he loved listening to me sing.

It was there at that church where I thought that I was totally healed of my mental illness. I stopped taking my medicine all at once! **Big mistake.** I was free from medication and happy to be set free from manic-depression, or so I thought at the time. Soon after I stopped taking the medication abruptly, my behavior began to change for the worse. I went into a full-blown manic state. This was another nightmare. Although I had gone peaceable into the ambulance before when I was depressed and needed help, this time I was less in control. There was no stopping me.

I was soon taking long walks outside in the snow without wearing a coat. My mind was once again in a manic state, and Joshua, who really DID help me when I was depressed, was at his wits' end. He attempted to keep me in the house because I talked to all the neighbors and they wondered what was wrong with me. Once I actually was being chased down the road by Joshua when I flew into a neighbor's house and ran into the back bedroom belonging to an old man in a wheelchair who was absolutely shocked to see me. I said "Don't move, Charlie, there's someone after me! Please protect me. Oh, Charlie, you are my only hope!" His wife had let Joshua in the front door to find me and he came into the back bedroom where I was crouched down on the floor behind Charlie and his bulky wheelchair. "Save me, Charlie!" The man in the wheelchair just sat there without saying a word. Maybe he couldn't say a word. Joshua could see that there was no way he was going to get me out of the house at the time and he probably had to go to work, so he left me there. In time, I crawled out and Charlie's wife, whom I had befriended long before, made something for me to eat. She was such a sweetheart. Looking back, it was quite comical that I found comfort from Charlie who couldn't believe I ran right into his back bedroom like that. It was probable that I was locked out of the house but in such a state of mind that I was unable to ask the neighbor for a ladder and crawl through the kitchen window.

Soon after this Joshua and I were standing in the driveway of our home and he was trying to convince me to get in the car and go to the hospital.. Joshua gave me a slap across the face as hard as he could and said "You're coming with me." I was stunned by the pain of the slap and somehow made the decision that Joshua was right, so I agreed to go to the hospital. Looking back, I am grateful that he got me the help I needed at the time.

I got into the car with Joshua and he quickly drove me to the local hospital. I cooperated at the emergency room. I signed all the forms and remember being taken into the psychiatric ward. I was experiencing some delusions. For example, I believed that my psychiatrist was a pimp and all the patients were prostitutes. I was placed in the "rubber room" at one point where there was nothing but a tiny window on the door so that the staff could look in to see if the person is okay in there. Who knows why they even check; when a person is in that room—he or she is NOT okay, no matter what. I felt like it was torture being left in a room like that all alone, not able to walk around much and nowhere to use the bathroom. I was seen every day by my psychiatrist and he kept telling my family that "she will come out of this eventually".

I was given Thorazine which made my mouth so dry that I was unable to talk or eat. I was suffering terribly as I walked around with my tongue with cracks and lesions on it and continually hurting. It was not until my sister Gini, the nurse in the family, came to see me and told the psychiatrist that I was malnourished and needed some Ensure to drink to get some vitamins and minerals every day. I also refused to take a shower or a bath, so Gini coaxed me into the tiny shower with her and bathed me, washing my hair and telling me everything would be alright.. Who knew how long it had been since I had gotten clean.

I believed that I was pregnant, as do a lot of women in that state of mind. Fortunately for me, I was not.

At every meal after this visit from Gini, I was offered an Ensure, a chocolate cold beverage that I was able to slowly drink through a straw. This felt so good going down my throat and I was thankful, even in my manic state, to have something to take away the misery of a swollen tongue.

One day I was sitting in Dr. Praseed's office when I heard him say, "She will just come out of this all at once." As soon as he said those words, I came back into reality. I looked around and realized where I was, and then looked down and saw I was wearing these cute little pink sweat pants and a flowered top that I didn't quite recognize. I looked at the doctor and asked, "Where did I get these clothes and what am I doing here?" Dr. Praseed was thrilled and knew that it was the beginning of the end of my delusions. He kept me in the hospital for a while after that just to make sure I was okay. Joshua was at a point where he had quit even trying to visit me because I was not being very nice to him while in this state of mind.

Slowly but surely I came back to reality and wanted out of the hospital. The day I was discharged I felt such a sense of freedom; I couldn't wait to get back into my life again. I had lost a lot of weight in the hospital and bought a tiny pair of jeans. I was wearing those jeans when I went to GE to visit my friend there. My friend was not very nice when I approached her and told me to go home and get well. She gave me some Bible Study material and basically told me not to return to the plant. I had no recollection of how I may have behaved with this woman prior to my hospital stay.

The torture of not being in my right mind for that period of time just took over my thought life with such a sense of shame. As time marched on I made new decisions about accepting my illness, and knew that it was okay. Over the years I had heard many times, "Remember, Nancy, God doesn't make junk." I hated when people said this because, in my mind, junk was something you found in a junkyard, not a person. It never made me feel any better about *my* situation.

What did make me feel better was along the same lines; I realized that God made my brain. And God does not make mistakes. All of us humans make mistakes; yes, even psychiatrists make mistakes, the mentally ill can surely make mistakes—but God? Absolutely not! Therefore, I now know that there has been a reason for all of the suffering I have endured in my lifetime. I believe we go through illnesses so that we can eventually help other people. My life mission is to help educate the world on what mental illness really is and give a better understanding to people who truly do not understand it. When I was in the manic state I felt invincible and had false pride. When I was depressed, it seemed there was no reason to live. That was two polar opposites. Never have I thought of murder or even physically hurting another human being; that is how the media portrays "us". The truth is, people diagnosed with mental illness of any kind are usually the victims, not the perpetrators. We are the ones who learn to live the best possible way we can while dealing with strange symptoms that appear out of nowhere and then disappear just as quickly. All I can say is that God is in control of my life and has made my life beautiful as I have grown over many years into a much more spiritual and mentally mature woman.

Chapter 12

Trumbull Homes

Joshua and I decided to get divorced after about two years of marriage. Joshua took everything out of the house that belonged to me and put it in the garage. I cleaned out the garage and put everything in storage, and then moved back into my parents' home. Because I was pulling in Social Security Disability I decided not to look for work, but instead, take on a play at Kent Branch. It was called, ironically, "Working". It was a musical and I got to sing! I had a good part and as time went on, the director gave me more and more parts and I enjoyed it immensely.

Eventually I felt that I didn't want to live at home and wanted to be on my own. My parents had retired and wanted to be on *their* own as well. It was then that I made the phone call to Trumbull Metropolitan Housing Authority and asked if I could be put on the waiting list for an apartment. I finally received a call back and was told that there was an opening at a government funded housing project called Trumbull Homes. I called the police and asked them if there were any gangs that lived there. In my utter innocence I listened to this police officer who told me that there was no such thing as gangs in Warren, Ohio.

I went and saw my apartment and thought it would be just fine for me to live in. After all, during the day there didn't seem to be much activity in the neighborhood. I drove to my newly found apartment in my Chevy Chevette and moved in with my belongings. It was better than paying for everything to be in storage. I lived for one full year at Trumbull Homes, and while the rent was only $50.00 a month, it was soon apparent that the environment was not safe. I learned a lot that year, especially about how to survive when surrounded by some—but not all—nasty, hateful, mean and scary people. My address was 2020 S. Project Drive.

Although I knew better than to befriend people there in the projects, it was so in my nature to be friendly. There was one woman named Jodi who had beautiful long blonde hair. She was married with two children and seemed like a nice person, so I hung out with her sometimes. I was thrilled when Jodi introduced me to her mother as the "normal one around here." I made friends with a lot of the little children who lived in the projects, among whom were two young sisters named Sissy and Missy, part of a family I had met while staying in Someplace Safe, a safe house for women. Their mother Dana called me every Sunday morning and told me it was "time to go to church." A big Baptist church bus used to pick them all up and drive them to a church in McDonald, Ohio. I gave in every time and joined the gang of children and a few adults on the bus ride to the church on Sunday mornings. I was glad that I didn't have to drive because it was kind of a long way to this church and, in time, I led the children in song while riding the bus.

I soon learned that Dana's ex-husband also lived at Trumbull Homes and I was warned to stay away from him. But instead of staying away from him, I befriended him, so in turn I was friends with Dana and her five children along with their father, Dana's ex-husband. I could never understand how these people hooked up with each other because they just seemed so different. Ernie was a major drug and alcohol user. He had this addiction so badly that there were times I didn't think he was going to live through his drunkenness.

Dana always said that one day he was going to go overboard and accidently overdose. I was so naive about drugs that I couldn't believe that could be possible. Ernie had a strong affection for me and we became pretty good friends, especially when I introduced him to Dr. Radeem, my first psychiatrist. Dr. Radeem, at the time, was getting a reputation as a Dr. Feel Good for all the local drug addicts. In fact, while sitting in his office waiting to be seen, I noticed there was a large number of drug addicted people sitting in his waiting room ready to get their "fix" of Ativan, Klonipin, or what have you. It was sad for me to realize that the drug addicts were taking full advantage of Dr. Radeem, and that his kindheartedness was getting him in more trouble than he was aware of. There was a time when Ernie was hospitalized in the Psych Ward just to get more drugs. He really didn't have a mental illness, and sometimes I would get mad at myself for even being friends with this creepy man. He was, like most guys I knew, a major B.S.er who would constantly compliment me about my beauty. I would listen to his compliments as he and a "visitor" would be engaged a drug deal and I sat in the kitchen oblivious as to what was happening right in front of me! (As a side note, Ernie eventually did die of an accidental overdose years later.)

Everyday Life at Trumbull Homes

With this in mind, I was outside one day sweeping my little cement walk when out of the blue a car screeched to a stop and this disheveled woman with straggly greasy hair and a big bouncing stomach leaped out of the passenger's side, came running up to me with her fists clenched and got right in my face. This woman, whom I'd never met before, called me every nasty name in the book and was sure that I was the one who had some kind of affair with her boyfriend. The anger just seethed through her and it was obvious that she intended to have a punched out fight. I suddenly felt a hedge of protection all around my body like a shield, giving me the peace of mind that this woman could not penetrate no matter how hard she tried. I also remained silent. I had never been in a fist fight with anyone and I surely wasn't going to fight over something that was a lie anyway. After what seemed like an eternity, the neighbors (a house full of five or six family members) came outside and said to the woman "I think you have the wrong person. I don't think it was her." As this furious woman backed off she was still yelling out cuss words as fast as she could, and then she finally turned and got back into the car. I was relieved, thanked the neighbors and went inside. It was then that I started shaking. "Thank you, Jesus, thank you, thank you, thank you." He had protected me from harm.

I was talked into having a Mary Kay party by a young woman from the Baptist Church named Carrie. She was very happy that I booked a party, but she had no idea where I lived. Because none of my real friends were really willing to visit me in this horrible neighborhood (and I didn't blame them), I gave out the invitations to four or five women who lived nearby, including Jodi, the married one with the two children. Well, I found out later that Jodi with the long blonde hair was a prostitute. She had been the one person who had introduced me to her mother as "the normal one around here". The other women who participated were drug addicts or had just plain made some wrong choices in life. If you think about it, something would have had to happen to make anyone end up in Trumbull Homes. With a rent of $50.00 a month it was obvious that no one had any money…including myself! So Carrie walked down the street pulling along all of her Mary Kay paraphernalia in a neat pink suitcase, and as she did there were whistles and hoots and hollering from the local men. When I answered the door the first thing she said was, "You gotta move out of this neighborhood, Nancy!" I laughed a little and agreed, and then we all sat down in my living room and enjoyed every minute of being pampered. Each woman applied a facial mask, gently washed it off, tried the make-up, each of us with our little Mary Kay mirrors that Carrie had provided, and we felt beautiful. We each received mascara to use and some foundation which was individually designed for each of our skin tones. She also had little "sample" lipsticks which the women were not shy to ask if they could keep them because, of course, once they were used, the person had no choice but to keep them. After about an hour and a half of this wonderful make-up party it was time for us to purchase something…anything…from Carrie's Mary Kay line. All the women, including myself, suddenly fell silent. Carrie stood there in disbelief. Not one woman made a purchase, and so Carrie packed up all of her beauty belongings, said her "good-byes," and left while the ladies slowly dispersed. Although this Mary Kay Representative may have been upset that she didn't make a single sale that night, she will never know how much worthwhile dignity she gave some of these ladies with just a few hours of respect and care for their beauty.

As I was literally shocked when I found out that my friend Jodi was a prostitute, I was even more shocked to wake up one morning and go outside only to see in big bold letters "TASK FORCE" on some of the doors of these homes. The first one I noticed was on Ernie's' front door. I wanted to know what this meant so I went over and knocked on Ernie's door. "Who is it?" I heard him yell. "It's me, Nancy." Ernie opened the door and he looked like a brick had hit him. He told me that there had been a raid after a selling of drugs to undercover cops, and that every person that had a "TASK FORCE" sign on the door was being evicted from their homes. I knew that Ernie may have done some drugs, which explained his inability to wake up sometimes, but I never thought that it was that big of a problem. I thanked God that I didn't happen to be visiting there when they had come to his house.

While I lived there at Trumbull Homes, there was an African American man who also owned a car, which was unusual, as almost everyone there did not. He was always in the parking lot working on his car when I would get home, and each time he saw me he yelled at the top of his lungs, "I love you!" I would yell back, "Me too, you!" And we would go our separate ways. In fact, I never spoke to him any other time, and I thought this little ritual we did was kind of funny. He, obviously had a good heart, as opposed to this other African American man whom I had met outside and ignorantly told him which apartment I lived in. This guy would come over each and every day at about the same time. I would hear his car rattling down the street and he would turn off the ignition right in front of my apartment. He would then proceed to bang on my front door over and over saying, "I know you are in there!" He was up to no good and I knew it. Each time he came around I would make sure my dead bolts were locked and hide in my living room and not make a sound. I was more or less living in fear all the time. There were many men and women who lived there who had "the look": The look of evil in their eyes.

One morning, I came out to my Chevy Chevette to go to the store and found that my car had been broken into and someone had tried to steal it. I called my father and he said, "That's it! You are moving out of that neighborhood!" It was then that my father and I went on a search for the perfect trailer for me to live in.

While we were searching for a trailer, my father had another idea in mind as to where I could live. He and I had gone outside his house one day, just walking through the property. He pointed to the end of their ranch home and told me that he was thinking of adding on to the house and would possibly have his son-in-law, Keith, build an extra apartment including a bathroom on the end of the house for me to live in. This way, we all would have privacy. I wasn't thinking real well at this point because I couldn't make any decisions, I just agreed with what my father said.

Looking back, I feel like crying when remembering all that my parents did for me and how much they loved me. If it had not been for them being a stable rock for me to turn to, I really do not think I would be here today. I once asked my mother why she never gave up on me and she replied "The thought never entered my mind!" I remember all the decisions that my father had made for me over the years of suffering with mental illness. He told me to go back to college and try again at the local Kent Branch, which I did and successfully got an Associate's Degree in Business. He told me to move to Rhode Island with my sisters and I did, which opened up a brand new life for me. He explicitly told me ***not*** to move to Hollywood to try to become famous. So I did not. My father was instrumental in helping me move on with life. The decisions that I made on my own seemed to cause me nothing but trouble.

111

Chapter 13

Flashbacks to a Nightmare

Making my own bad decisions was never more apparent than when I was living in Rhode Island. Back then I lived with such an inferiority complex that most of the time I just thought my life wasn't worth living. Tombstones were my friends and I spent a lot of time in cemeteries no matter where I was living. The cemeteries seemed peaceful to me, and at the time, with absolutely no religious affiliation, I believed that I would eventually be just that: a tombstone. So, this is where danger could loom because I would do anything for acceptance. One night in 1986, while I was living in Rhode Island, but before I met Max, I was at a busy bar in downtown Providence. This man was there who I thought was one of the best looking men I had ever laid eyes on. He was different, and when he spoke he had a thick European accent which was even more enticing to me. What I did not see were the horns and long scaly tail that he had. As alluring as he was, he was even more demonic. Looking back, I can see where I made my mistake, but at the time I fell right into his trap. I had never met anyone quite like him. Lust just poured from his being. His hair, his eyes, his strong build and his sexy accent were so attractive. His words were as smooth as the alcohol he bought me as he lit my cigarettes. His eyes seemed to pour into my very soul. He asked me if we could get together the next evening since he had to go right then, leaving on some other kind of mission. I agreed, and as crazy as it sounds, we planned to go to a hotel the next night. I went to work that day in an excited frenzy. This guy was more than something to look forward to because of his demeanor and his magnetic charm that exuded from him as he talked and stared at me. I felt like this was going to be quite the night to remember, meeting up with this man whose name I still can't remember. He had asked me if I could pick him up and gave me an address. When I was getting ready to leave the house where I lived with my sister and her husband, my brother-in-law was sensing something was wrong and stopped me in the living room. He said, "Be careful tonight, Nan." I thought it strange as he had never said anything like this before. That should have been my first warning.

I found the road he lived on and picked him up in the dark. He then directed me to drive until we came upon a small hotel, meanwhile mentioning that he was out of money, so I would have to pay for the evening. He sounded sincere enough as he promised he would pay me back the next time he saw me. Soon I found myself lying in bed while the man took a long shower. I was starting to get a really bad vibe from him when he grabbed me into his arms and took my body over with a force and roughness that I had never experienced before. He pulled my head up and slammed it down on the back of the headboard, immediately sending a warning fear throughout my being like an alarm was going off and I tried desperately to get away from him. He just was so relentless and powerful I felt like a ragdoll being tossed to and from all over the bed. The pain was excruciating, the room was spinning, and he pulled my head up several more times and hit my head on the back of the headboard. I didn't have time to scream nor was I able to. I finally passed out and could remember no more of the night. The last thing I do remember was asking him how many women had he done this to and he replied, "Hundreds and hundreds." I kept hearing his thick accent saying those words over and over as my head reeled and my body was screaming in pain.

When I finally came to, I looked at the clock and knew I already was late for work. I had brought my work outfit just in case the night would turn into morning, but nothing could have prepared me for this. I got up and went into the bathroom looking at my naked body. I had bruises and marks all over my body and had a painful stab of pain coming from within. The back of my head was hurting also. I stared at myself and then got into the shower, knowing that it was the same shower that this monster had used early in the evening. The hotel soap smelled like him. I was too upset to cry. Actually, I was so ashamed that I didn't feel I deserved to cry. I got out of the shower and dressed for work because, after all, that is where I belonged and that was where I had to go. When I got to work there was a woman who demanded that I type up her loan before any others. I could not think, nor type, nor breathe correctly; I was in shock and in so much pain. After already being late, within a few hours I knew I was unable to produce any work that day. I apologized to the woman who needed my help and told my boss I must go home. I made it home and curled up in my bed, shaking. I felt so shameful and guilty and stupid that death seemed like the only way out, as usual. I had paid for the hotel! I had asked for it!

I never told anyone about this rape until the year 2007 because I hid it in the deepest place in my heart and mind. I did, however, tell my mother a little bit about it when I came for a visit to Ohio. My mother forced me to make an appointment at St. Joseph's Riverside Hospital for a HIV test. I was so embarrassed to have this done, and it did not seem very private—as if everyone in the waiting room knew what the test was for. Thank God the test was negative, although at the time I didn't care. Aids or HIV would just be a quicker route to death and being a comforting tombstone in the cemetery of my choice.

The reason for this "flashback," per say was that there were plenty of men who lived near and around Trumbull Homes that I could feel a bad vibe from. Now, knowing the Lord, He helped me figure out who was okay to be with and who was not. I learned everything the hard way, it seemed. It soon was apparent that the only time it was safe to be outside while living in Trumbull Homes was during the day. I would lie in bed and hear gunshots at night. I felt safe in my bed with the wires on the windows and with the Lord Jesus to always protect me, but I also knew that I had to be very careful about whom I would let in as a friend. I did find a friend named Josephine, an older African American lady who lived across the street in a bungalow. Josephine and I became very close and exchanged phone numbers early on. I would spend a lot of time over at Josephine's house talking about the Lord. She had a beautiful statue of Jesus in her living room— He was African American! I thought that it was really cool that Josephine believed that Jesus was African American. Anyway, Josephine and I became very close, and when we were watching Jeopardy in our separate homes, I would call her on the phone with the Jeopardy answer and laugh, and then hang up. Josephine counted on me to take her to the store and I counted on her to keep me accountable as a Christian.

Chapter 14

Changes

I had gotten a little kitten that I named Jose, and this little kitty became extremely important to me. I named him after my favorite doctor. He just was a nice little male cat that purred a lot and kept me company. I taught Jose how to go up and down the steps and we spent many hours together. When Jose got bigger I had him spayed and took great care of him. He was to stay inside my house and not go out into the scary world of Trumbull Homes where even a cat could get into trouble. One day, however, someone came to my door and when I opened it, Jose snuck out. I was on high alert chasing after my cat as fast as I could. The cat was running at top speed and soon there were many young kids chasing Jose too, which made Jose run even faster. I kept calling Jose and suddenly it seemed that children were coming out of everywhere chasing after him and yelling, "Jose!" It seemed to take forever but finally I got my cat. I held him tight as I walked back to my home. The poor cat was so out of breath I was worried about him. Once he got back into the house it took a while for the cat to start breathing normally. This incident reminded me, again, how important it was to keep Jose, along with my own self sometimes, safe inside the house.

One night I woke up thirsty in the middle of the night as the medication that I was taking made me incredibly thirsty all the time. As I walked down the stairs toward the kitchen, I slipped and fell, tumbling all the way down the stairs. The glass I was carrying broke and cut my hand in two places, bleeding profusely. I called 911 and for the first time experienced the stigma of living in government housing. The ambulance took forever; it seemed, to get there. The EMT's were not very friendly and actually acted as though I was a nuisance and not worthy of being treated with respect because of my address. The ambulance took me to the local hospital where a surgeon happened to be working that evening and asked me if he could do the honors of stitching my wrist. I wasn't sure how to take this doctor—could he be flirting with me, or just showing pity? Anyway, he stitched up my wounds very carefully and I called a friend to take me home. I had a few bandages wrapped around my wrist and the surgeon said he wanted to see me again. He gave me his card and I followed up with the appointment. He really was a well-known surgeon in the area and I was glad that he did a good job with my stitches after being treated so badly by the EMT.

While attending a new Baptist church I joined the choir right away. Singing was always something that I felt good about, and after my conversion I would remain steadfast to the call on my life to sing Gospel and Gospel only. It wasn't really a choice; it was just something that happened within me. I realized that in heaven the only songs that would be sung would be to glorify Jesus. I also had noticed early on that when I sang a song about Jesus, my voice was clearer and stronger than when I sang secular songs. All those years of singing every sexy tune on the radio were over for me. The other interesting thing that happened was…I could not go to a bar. It was also one of those things that were not by choice, but I was fine with it. Walking into a bar would open three doors that needed to stay shut forever. 1. Men 2. Alcohol and 3. Cigarettes. Just to know that there was some control over these three areas assisted me at the beginning of my journey of finding "self-control." It wasn't until I had many therapy sessions with the best pastors I had ever met that I totally gave up men completely, not needing or wanting one in my life. That was such a freedom from bondage! It took a number of years but I also made two other decisions. One was to try to quit drinking alcohol all together, and that suicide was not an option. No! Not ever!

There were so many freedoms that I experienced from learning what the Bible says, having excellent counsel, and befriending wise Christian women…the kind that I used to despise for so long, thinking they were "goodie two-shoes". People think that when they become a Christian they have to change everything *themselves* and that they will not be "cool" or have any fun if they give Jesus their life. That is absolutely not true! In fact it is the opposite. I did not change myself; the God of the universe was changing me and bettering my life day by day as I followed Him implicitly.

There is something that is very important to mention that was always preached in this Baptist church. It was a very straight forward message that simply said, "When you give your life to Jesus, you know that you *know* that you **know**… that you will be going to heaven when you die. That is something to totally rejoice about! Unfortunately, if you choose not to give your life to Jesus, you will not be going to heaven when you die, but to a place called hell where there will be fire and loneliness and emotional and physical pain forever and ever. Over the years I studied about hell in the Bible, and it is true. People do not believe that hell is real, and they don't care to think about it. I say that if heaven and hell *are* real, wouldn't you want to be sure where you are going… just in case? Many people do not commit suicide because they are afraid that God would send them to hell. Whether true or not true (I do not know), it is a good reason for people to decide not to do it.

For those of you who are reading with an attitude of non-belief, let me honestly tell you; not only do you get the promise of heaven, but while you are alive you can become best friends with the Maker of the universe. He is with you always and only wants good things to happen to you. As I've experienced, your life can change for the good. My joy is not from mania. It is the joy of the Lord. I will thank Him until the day I die and get to see Him, Jesus, my best friend. God is love. If you ever wondered where love came from, it was not a manmade emotion. God is love. I am learning to love with God's unconditional love. It is nonjudgmental and pure.

A New Place to Call Home

My father and I finally found a nice trailer for me to live in that was located in Cortland not far from my parents' house. My sister Chris and her husband Keith got his family together and as I walked around in a numb state, they moved me out of my Trumbull Homes apartment and into my new trailer. I thank God for what they did for me that day.

It was the year 1996 and I began going to the church that I would have gone the morning that I gave my life to Jesus, but I was not sure where it was. I had known that North-Mar Church was where I would inevitably make my church home. The first Sunday that I was there, I went up to the choir director and told him I would like to join the choir. He was one of the nicest persons I had ever met. His name was Jim Garber. I went to choir practice that very week and was excited that I could sing in their Christmas Cantata. There were so many nice ladies in the choir who took me under their wing and asked me out for coffee and/or welcomed me into their homes. I felt loved and was not afraid to share my story of living with—as they now call it—bipolar disorder. Although my confidence still faltered, the people were so kind to me that I sometimes felt overwhelmed with the joy of the Lord. It was different from being manic. It was coming from the heart instead of the head.

The true test came one Wednesday evening at choir practice. There just wasn't enough room in the choir loft for the growing number of choir members, so Jim Garber had a few of us in the front use fold out chairs. There I was in the front row at a choir practice trying to open my folding chair and facing the entire choir. As I tugged and pulled on this chair, I just couldn't get it to open, and without thinking I yelled "SHIT!" loud and clear for everyone to hear. Mind you, I was facing the choir when this happened. I looked around the choir with more ***attitude*** than embarrassment. I thought "Okay, just tell me that none of you swear!" Each person was looking in different directions pretending that they didn't hear what I said. Some were looking at each other with a smirk. I thought to myself that if anyone judged me, like it says in the Bible, let he who has no sin throw the first stone! I've never forgotten that no stones were thrown, so to speak, and that the ladies in the choir made even more of an effort to help me.

Although I was 34 years old, my maturity level had stayed at about 18 years old when I was first diagnosed with bipolar disorder. Therefore, I liked to hang out with the young girls in the choir and act silly. Jim Garber, the choir director, was about five years older than me, but I thought of him as a father figure and a mentor. I would tell Jim when I would get sloppy drunk (yes, I had not quit drinking altogether yet) and ask him to pray for me as the guilt of drinking began taking on a new light. I really did begin to feel guilty about this, so I would drink less often, but still get sloppy drunk when I did drink. Jim was always there to pray with me and it seemed that when he prayed, all my burdens were lifted. Soon I learned the scripture "A righteous man's prayers availed much." I thought of Jim as being one of the most righteous men I had ever met. He was filled with the love of the Lord and he was friendly and kind with everyone. He loved the choir like a family and used to say, "I hope my mansion in heaven is near all of yours." He had years and years of wisdom from the Bible that I just wanted to soak up. I told him about all the suicide attempts and emotional pain that I had endured for so many years. Jim was a great listener and friend. His wife and two sons were nice enough to allow me to talk to him and maybe hold up what they were planning as a family that day or what have you. I thanked God that I was fitting in well with the people at North-Mar church and enjoying great teaching through Sunday school and the sermons.

After about a year a family came to live in Howland, Ohio from Chicago. Myron and Sharon had four children, all young boys.

Pastor Myron was a gifted counselor with a degree in Psychology as well as his Theology degree. I was in a really bad relationship with a man named Rick and needed to get out of it. The man I was dating cursed like a sailor, smoked marijuana, and although he was kind to me, he was hateful and notorious for telling people off and wanting to get revenge. I wanted to stay away from this man but the temptation to be with him was overwhelming. One day when I was in this man's home, I actually saw a demon. It had scaly skin and long claw-like fingers and the demon was side by side next to this man, showing me that he represented a demon. The interesting thing was that I was not afraid of the demon and didn't tell the man that I saw it. I did feel it was time to come clean with this relationship and to get some help to end it. When people talk about being unequally yoked, this man was tipping the scales of being on the opposite side of where my spirit was. I use to tell him about the Lord and even gave him a Bible, but he thought it was all hogwash. One time when I was singing a Christian song that I loved, this man began cursing with every word he could think of. When I asked what was wrong, he said that he couldn't stand the song. It was really time to move on. I felt I was in the fight of my life to get Rick out of my life!

Transformation

I made an appointment to see Pastor Myron for some counsel concerning men. The morning that I was to go talk to Myron, I had the most difficult time getting ready and out the door. I felt as though there was some unknown force holding me back. I ended up being late for the appointment but was glad that I even made it there. Pastor Myron had a way of cutting to the chase. He asked me what was happening with this man I was involved with and I told him what his character was like but how hard it was to stay away from him. Without worry that he may have thought that I was crazy, I told Myron about seeing the demon, but that I wasn't scared because I knew that the demon represented this man and I wasn't afraid of HIM. Without blinking an eye, Pastor Myron stated, "Nancy, God revealed that demon to you for a reason. He is trying to tell you that this man is not the one for you and you really need to stay away from him completely." I felt a sense of peace come over me as Pastor Myron and I prayed, repenting not just for my sexual sin with this man but for my sexual sin ever since I gave my life to the Lord. You see, the Bible talks about sexual sin as not just a physical act, but that of two spirits bonding together. It can be poisonous to someone who has given their life to the Lord and their body to Him as a living sacrifice – the body becomes God's pure temple but is violated by fornication outside the institute of marriage (Cor. 3:16 and 6:18-20). I remembered men from my past and I prayed to be set free from the bondage of sexual sin. And I *was* set free from the emotional dependence on men and set free from lust and all that went with it. The longer I prayed with Pastor Myron, the more peace I felt inside.

Although the meeting was almost entirely about men, I was set free from every stronghold that the devil had established within me. The mania, the depression, and the behaviors that these "illnesses" had brought on were being broken. I realized for the first time that mania was not something that gave me a license to sin and do whatever I wanted, as the psychiatrists suggested. When I would become manic, the psychiatrists would encourage me to "have a good time," or even say, 'I'm sure your boyfriend will enjoy your mania." Mania and promiscuous behavior go hand in hand, and for years I felt I was justified as a "sick" person to do what I wanted without a care in the world. I knew the truth, but just couldn't seem to follow it. This was an eye-opening experience for me. Although I wasn't thinking that it was right to have sex outside of marriage, I was used to that behavior and encouraged by professionals to behave as if I had no control over myself. I was now disgusted with the thought of being so out of control sexually which I had been brainwashed into thinking was okay.

I learned that the idea of lust was not from God. When two who belong to Him are married and they join together, it is a beautiful thing that He was totally responsible for originating. There is no "lust," because Jesus is there in the room. But to the world, the devil has distorted the meaning of the act into the selfishness of lust.

I was amazed that 'the peace beyond all understanding' had filled my entire being. I had never felt closer to my Jesus and was filled with joy, peace, grace, and love…it was similar to the time that Jesus came down like a blanket of love when I was in Rhode Island during that suicide attempt. This was actually even a stronger love that permeated throughout my soul. When I finally said my good-byes to Pastor Myron, I walked out of his office feeling so much peace and contentment that I thought I was weightless, just floating down the hallway of the church offices. I left there a changed woman. I was set free from every chain that bound me to sin. It was phenomenal.

What happened next may have scared the average person but I recognized what was happening and decided to laugh it off. It is better to laugh at the devil then to fear him. Satan was so angry that I was set free from this bondage of sexual sin that I was suddenly bombarded for the next three days (or longer) by men literally knocking at my front door, calling me on the phone, asking for my phone number at the grocery store, and attracting old friends, new friends and even enemies from my past. All of whom were male! I called Pastor Myron and discussed it with him as well as with some strong faith- filled Christian women who also agreed I should laugh at all the circumstances the devil was putting me in. I was laughing as I hid on the floor of my bedroom when there were knocks at my front door. I would sneak a peek out the front curtain and it never failed to be a man that I once knew. The real kicker was a phone call from a man who had chased me days after I had given my life to the Lord. This guy was so filled with lust I had to literally fight him off. He had claimed to be an atheist and certainly was. Although he denied any religious affiliation, I saw a big cross up at his house. When I asked him about it he said that he sometimes felt demons in his house, so he thought if he put a cross up they would go away. I was warned in a dream that if I slept with him I would get pregnant. I dreamt that I should call the baby "Thomas" after his father. I didn't know what that meant because this man's name was not

Thomas. As I woke up and got to thinking, I suddenly remembered seeing his college diploma up on his wall and his real first name was Thomas, but he went by his middle name. What a warning! As it was, he had gotten someone pregnant and had married them many years earlier. Just knowing that this man called me after all these years and left a message on my answering machine that simply stated he was "thinking of me" was profound. I also went to see my psychiatrist during those three days. When I walked into the waiting room, there was another one! This man had been chasing after me the last time I had been in the psychiatric ward. He was quite a handsome dude, but another one filled with lust. He asked me for my phone number and I just shook my head.

The devil was losing, as he does lose in the end, so that is why he tries so hard when he knows it is an opportune time. Yes, the devil was losing and I was laughing, except when it came to Rick. I became obsessed with Rick. Each time I would sit down to read the Bible I kept thinking "I have to call Rick. I have to call Rick." Pastor Myron was on hand to help me through this break-up, but it was definitely one of the most difficult things I had ever had to do.

As far as I was concerned I had a brand new boyfriend—one who would never hurt me but would always be with me, side by side. His name was Jesus and He was very close indeed, living inside of me, actually. Pastor Myron told me to "flee from temptation," as the Bible says. I asked what exactly that meant and he told me to literally get up and RUN from it! So when Rick came over or called I had to tell him it was over. I could see the pain in his eyes and I couldn't stand to hurt him, but I actually had to think of him as an enemy. It was really hard. The more I tried to stay away from him, the more I wanted to be with him. He had this charisma that just pulled me, lured me, and went against every fiber of my being. I was in a true battle. I broke down and ended up at his house. As we sat on his couch watching TV, Rick began making the moves on me and I had to fight for my life right there on his couch. He was really confused and could not understand what had happened to me. I tried to explain it but it was just not something he was able to comprehend. I was having a hard time saying no to him. I suddenly remembered what Pastor Myron said: "RUN!" I leaped off the couch, ran out his front door and kept on running as fast as I could. Rick was yelling at the top of his lungs "What the hell's the matter with you?"

More Good News

With the newfound knowledge of having Jesus as my boyfriend, I felt sure that Pastor Myron was correct in saying that I would one day meet a Christian man and I would get married again, only this time it would be for keeps. I honestly didn't care if I stayed single for the rest of my life because I felt I had it all. With Jesus as my boyfriend I could never go wrong again and I really didn't think much about getting married again. Unbeknownst to me, many of the women I had befriended in the choir were praying for me to find a man to marry. I was taught that God prepares a man and He prepares a woman and gets them to just the right place where they need to be to meet and enjoy a deep friendship and then get married... without sex prior to marriage. I thought this would be great for someone else, but I liked being single. I didn't have to answer to anyone and could come and go when I pleased. I had plenty of friends and three cats as well. (Jose now had a brother and a sister, Pepper and Petunia.) I felt very content with where I was in my life. I was receiving benefits from Social Security, paying my $133 lot fee at the trailer park and enjoying myself. It seemed as though each day brought more and more stability with my moods as I started to mature both mentally and spiritually.

I was thriving there at the small trailer park, making friends with all the neighbors, especially the elderly ones. I became very close to an old man by the name of Al. He had a John Deere push mower and asked me if I would consider mowing his lawn. I agreed wholeheartedly without knowing what I was getting myself into. Al was a perfectionist and watched as I mowed his postage stamp yard. He wanted each line to be straight, and in return all he asked was for me not to run over his tomato plants. I learned quickly to mow perfectly, just as Al taught me. Soon other elderly people in the neighborhood were asking if I could mow their lawns. There I was in my 30's, and I had a lawn mowing business! I wasn't embarrassed about it; after all, I was on disability.

I always disliked the term "trailer trash," but as I noticed that most of the people in the park did not put their garbage cans back up for a few days after garbage collection night, that made the park look horrible. So each morning after the trash was collected, I would get up extra early and go around the park pulling up garbage can after garbage can and leaving them where I had noticed they were kept by their owner. I also became very close to Lynn, my next door neighbor, and we would talk for hours. She was probably 30 years my senior and also suffered from depression along with her sister, Mary, who had been involved in the outpatient unit with me. Although Mary came very close to dying from a serious suicide attempt, she lived through that but passed away one day just walking along when suddenly her heart gave out. Lynn and I became extremely close and I loved spending time with her in her neatly organized trailer. One thing that I remember about Lynn is that she refused to gossip. I never heard her say one nasty word about anyone in the park, no matter what they did. I loved her because of her values and her love for me, too.

I really did not spend a lot of time at home; instead, I would make my rounds befriending people in the park. One man, named Frank, was an elderly man who had absolutely no religious beliefs at all. I used to go over, mow his yard, then sit and talk with him for hours. I would tell him about the love of God and how He had totally changed my life from the inside out. I loved Frank and his little dog, Peanut. I also got to know his son who was into doing drugs and truly hated his father. It seemed like Frank wasn't happy with his son either. After I met his son, Tom, it seemed as though I would see him everywhere I went. God knew that we had to have a friendly relationship with each other so that Tom could trust me taking care of his father.

I started noticing that Frank, who sat in his lazy boy and watched TV all day long, was not feeling well. Each week when I went over to visit, it seemed that he was getting worse. One day Frank told me that he couldn't take care of his little dog, Peanut, anymore. I announced at choir practice that there was an adorable little dog weighing about six pounds that needed a home. The woman who took Peanut gave him to her relative in Florida, so to this day, little Peanut lives in the sunshine state. Finally Frank went into the hospital. I didn't really know what was wrong with him but I was there when he returned from the hospital. He was angry. He didn't want anyone to take care of him; he wanted to be able to take care of himself.

But I quickly realized that Frank was very sick and that he probably didn't have a lot of time left on this earth. Hospice was called in, a hospital bed was installed, and drugs like morphine were in the refrigerator to be administered to Frank. Frank's son, Tom, wanted to be in charge of the drugs, which was fine with me. One Saturday I asked Tom if I could stay with Frank all day, and he was glad for the respite. As Frank lay in the hospital bed so close to death, I felt it was time to see if he would want to make sure that he was going to heaven when he died. Just as this thought crossed my mind, a neighbor from across the street came knocking on the door. It was a dear Christian lady whom I had befriended months before. Knowing Frank was ill, she had stopped by to bring a casserole over. I immediately asked her to come in and told her that I was going to ask Frank if he would like to be sure he was going to heaven when he died. At this point, I said in a loud voice, as I knew that Frank was hard of hearing, "Frank, Frank, can you hear me?" Frank squeezed my hand. The neighbor took my other hand as I began to pray. Then I asked Frank if he would like to know that he is going to heaven when he dies. Frank nodded yes. I led him through the sinner's prayer and Frank murmured each word. Afterward, the neighbor and I rejoiced, knowing that the Bible tells us that the angels in heaven also rejoice each time a person gives their life to Jesus. That afternoon Frank's son came back to stay with his father. I went back to my trailer and prayed. In the morning I got an early call at 7:00 AM. It was Tom stating that Frank had passed away. I was kind of shocked because he was aware the day before and seemed content.

The night after Frank died, I had a supernatural experience. I went to bed praying and praying for a sign from God that Frank did make it into heaven. I actually received knowledge from God that Frank made it to heaven and I felt a sense of peace flood my spirit. I sang "Amazing Grace" at Frank's funeral. What an awesome God we serve!

Now my friend Al from down the road was also not doing so well. He was suffering from emphysema which is like a very slow death. Ever since I knew him, he was on oxygen, carrying a cumbersome tank wherever he went. Al told me that every single night he prayed for me to find a job that I really loved. He prayed a lot for me and as rough around the edges as he was, he helped me more than I would like to admit since I always thought I was helping Al. In time, my buddy Al passed away too.

One day, I was driving down the road in a near-by town called Champion when I saw a sign for a hairdresser named Lil Audrey which said "Walk-In's Welcome." I decided to stop and see if she was available to give me a much needed haircut. Lil Audrey graciously took me in and we had a wonderful conversation about the Lord as she was a very faith-filled Christian. I enjoyed her so much that I made her my official hairdresser. I liked the way she cut my hair and I began to really love her as a person. One afternoon as Lil Audrey was blow drying my hair, she told me that she knew of a man who I would possibly like to go out with. Lil Audrey told me that his name was Gary and that he was a musician. I was not interested since I had just gone through a learning experience and didn't want to date anyone. After talking with Lil Audrey awhile, I agreed to meet Gary Montagna at Perkins Restaurant after a Wednesday night choir practice. She had told me that there would be many single Christians meeting at her church and perhaps I could meet him, along with the other singles, after a Wednesday night choir practice. I went to choir practice and my friends were praying for me as I left and drove to Perkins. I had chosen to wear a flowered one-piece pantsuit that I had never worn before to look nice for Gary.

Lil Audrey and I sat at the table waiting for the others to come. Finally four men walked in together plus a little seven-year-old girl. I looked at each one, wondering which one was Gary. I soon found out it was the short one with messy dark hair. I was cordial to all of them but didn't get much of a chance to talk to Gary. Gary was not impressed with me in the least for two main reasons; he hated my flowered pantsuit and he thought that I was shaking because I was nervous. He didn't know at the time that I took Lithium which made my hands tremble at all times.

That Sunday, as Gary tells it, he was sitting in church praying about whether to ask me out again, kind of agonizing over it, when suddenly a woman whom he had never met before came up to him and said, "Whatever you are praying about, the answer is yes." (This is what happens in a charismatic type church and is called "a word of knowledge." When a person receives a word of knowledge from God, it is important to be bold enough to tell the person according to God's timing, not ours). With that knowledge, Gary called me on the phone for the first time and was in the middle of explaining his deepest theological beliefs when suddenly I said, "I have to go." Gary was confused and asked me, "Why?" and I replied, "I have to do my laundry." So we both hung up the phone leaving Gary confused and a bit ticked off. I awoke again at 11:00 PM and decided to call him back. When he answered I told him how sorry I was, it wasn't that I had to do my laundry but that I had to go to sleep. I took meds every night and I had already taken them. Somehow we ended up laughing about it, and so began the relationship between Gary and me. There was a continual stream of humor during the first few years of knowing each other. We both were the exact same age, 36, but both were immature and acted silly. I laughed more those first few months than I had laughed in my entire life. Gary was hilarious and so much fun to be around. We had met in October of 1998. We soon became best friends, even through the storm of two medical nightmares that suddenly hit a month and a half after we met.

Chapter 15

Multiple Sclerosis Diagnosis

I went to bed one night and woke up in the morning with not one cat laying on the bed, but two cats. I do not mean that there were really two cats on my bed, although I had three. I was seeing double. I saw a cat on the bed and then saw the same cat three feet above it, along with everything else in the room. I was scared. I was experiencing a bad case of double vision. Everywhere I went and everything I did, I saw double. There was two of everything! I called my psychiatrist who recommended me to go to his eye doctor, Dr. Pine. I went, only to see double everything on his screen. Dr. Pine did give me an eye patch to wear so that I would only see one of everything which made it easier to drive. Although I was upset at this development, I went to choir practice wearing the eye patch. Jim Garber even made a little joke about it, and I was glad that he did. It made the fear less overwhelming.

My family called and made an appointment for me at the Cleveland Clinic. In the meantime, I was scheduled for an MRI and the results were to be sent up to the clinic for a diagnosis. The prognosis did not sound promising. I was told that it was either a brain tumor or multiple sclerosis. Pastor Myron came to the local hospital where I sat in the waiting room with my mother waiting to have the MRI done. Pastor Myron prayed for me and gave me a Bible verse to meditate on during the procedure. I was so thankful that he came because it made me feel better about what was about to take place. After the MRI, I had an appointment at the Cleveland Clinic the day before Thanksgiving in 1998. The results from the MRI showed lesions on my brainstem; therefore I was diagnosed with multiple sclerosis.

On Thanksgiving Day our family was all together at my sister's house. My brother-in-law had printed out everything on the internet about MS, and as I was reading all these horrible reports of what happens to a person with MS—like becoming wheelchair or bed bound from the Mylar sheath disintegrating in the nerve cells—the fear inside me was building. Just the thought of my physical body deteriorating now...when I had finally found the real purpose of life and after all those suicide attempts seemed so bizarre. I was having a very difficult time trying to process it all, or to even believe it. In the meantime, Gary, too, was feeling ill and had to go to the doctor. He was diagnosed with ulcerative colitis around the same time as my diagnosis of MS. The future did not look bright for either of us.

I went to church that Sunday and walked down the steps to the choir room to get my robe on and prepare to line up with the choir. I was walking around paralyzed, not with the MS, but with intense fear and I was experiencing the inability to sing. For the first time since I got saved, I did not sing in the choir. Instead, I stayed downstairs there on the floor of the choir room just sobbing in emotional anguish. Again, I felt as though I was at a place where no one could help me and all the people I told about the illness had no answers for me. One woman sympathetically grabbed my hand in the church restroom during that time and prayed that God would get me through this "thorn in my flesh." This was a pastor's wife and it was the worst prayer that she could ever have prayed for me. For the last 20 some years my bipolar disorder had been explained away as a "thorn in my flesh." This phrase comes from the book of II Corinthians where Paul asked God three times to take away his thorn in the flesh, but God told him that His grace was sufficient, and that His strength would be revealed through Paul's weakness. This "thorn," or "messenger from Satan," kept Paul humble when he could have become proud about getting such revelation from God that he was able to write 2/3rds of the New Testament.

I was filled with such confusion. Was I really going to end up in a wheelchair unable to walk? The ladies at church prayed for me and that did help a lot, but it was not the disease itself that was bothering me as much as the intense fear. I knew I had to get rid of that. I also knew that I had to stop talking about the illness because people are literally ignorant when it comes to this kind of thing. I believe, on the whole, it is just our human nature that makes us say hurtful things like: "My uncle's brother-in-law had MS and died from it after spending 25 years in bed…but, I am praying for you." …Gee, thanks.

I was at home alone not long after this dreaded diagnosis and finally decided to ask Jesus what I was supposed to do about this diagnosis of MS and the wretched fear that went with it. While I was fervidly praying, I heard "Stand Firm!" loud and clear in my spirit. I went to my Bible and hand copied each and every scripture that said "Stand Firm," and there are a lot of them! In the book of Isaiah it states "Stand Firm or you will not stand at all!" That one really got me thinking. I had to trust Jesus with this illness and keep standing. I also went up to the altar on Communion Sunday at North-Mar Church and the elders gathered around me and anointed me with oil, just as it states to do in the book of James. When I was prayed for while on my knees at the altar, I suddenly felt two sensations: a burning hot flame in the back of my neck area, and then I felt my body relax and kind of slump back on the floor. When the Holy Spirit is at work and He is so powerful that the person just falls down, that is called being "slain in the Spirit." Although it normally happens in a charismatic type church, it can happen anywhere that the power of the Holy Spirit manifests itself.

I felt the MS leave me that day and was able to take off my eye patch. My friend Rhoda was there and said, "I knew you would get

133

healed!" It was a wonderful day for me, and I'll hold on to the words "Stand Firm" for the rest of my life.

Later on, in 2001, I started going tanning three days a week to have a nice suntan for my wedding. It was then that I noticed strong tingling and discomfort in my left arm and hand. I had forgotten what the doctors had told me and what I had read about MS. Heat is an absolute no-no for MS because it exacerbates it. I started to really get concerned when the feeling in my left hand slowly began leaving completely and I began feeling a strange type of pain in my left hand and arm. Unfortunately, I kept my tanning appointments until I realized what I had done, but it was too late! I believe that I had used my own free will in this case and because of it, I brought these symptoms on myself.

This time, I went to St. Elizabeth Hospital's MS clinic. I was assigned a doctor who sat me down in his office and told me he thought I should be on an antidepressant medication. I wanted to scream! All those years of antidepressants...did he not read my chart? I already HAD a psychiatrist! He began writing a prescription for Paxil. I politely told him that Prozac was my antidepressant of choice, so he changed it to Prozac. I reluctantly brought him the X-rays of my brain stem that showed the lesions on it that gave me this heartbreaking diagnosis. He then asked me to have another MRI just to see if the lesions had gotten worse. I agreed, and when I went back to see him, he was shocked. There were no lesions on my brain stem! Gone! In Jesus' name! He was puzzled. He then asked me to have yet another MRI of my spinal cord. In the meantime I had to sit in the waiting room filled with people who were in wheelchairs. One person said to me "What are your symptoms?" I told him. He stated confidently, "Oh! Yes, we all used to be like you...it only progresses." That was encouraging!

Gary came with me to the next appointment. The third MRI showed a tiny dot of a lesion on my spinal cord, and the doctor seemed to be so pleased that he found something. The spot was so small, yet proved to this neurologist that he, indeed, had a patient with MS. Again, I was given information about the shots I could give myself for the remainder of my life to try to slow down the progress of the disease. Again, I politely said "No" to this $2,000 a month procedure.

I began seeing this doctor on a regular basis and honestly, I did not like him at all. It was always the same thing…he would hit my knees with a little blunt object to see my reflexes then ask me numerous questions about my body. I kept telling him it was just my left hand—it was numb and it hurt in a strange kind of way.

At one such visit, my doctor told me to follow him into another room which looked like a type of lounge where the neurologists took their break or ate lunch. There were two doctors sitting there when my doctor brought me in and said, "Look at *my* patient, doctors. She was diagnosed in '98." They were very cordial to me, but I was not going to have this doctor get any credit! I told all three of them that I have a strong faith in God and His healing power and that is why I am doing so well.

That was the last time I ever saw a neurologist.

Gary, on the other hand, was not doing so well with his ulcerative colitis. After his diagnosis, he went to a gastroenterologist and was put on medication. The doctors said that it had nothing to do with his diet and everything to do with having a disease. (We later learned otherwise.) Gary and I were both told by physicians to "stay away from stress." That was easy for me because Gary made me laugh each and every day. As time went by, I was falling deeply in love with him. He was so very kind and exceptionally handsome to me.

The best part of my relationship with Gary was what the world would say was absolutely strange, but Gary and I knew that in God's eyes it was the right direction to follow. We abstained from having sex even though we had no idea that we were going to get married at that time. We prayed to God a lot to help us with this, knowing that it was what God wanted. So it was by us both making the decision and also asking for God's divine help that we were able to do it. Or should I say, not do it. After all, having Jesus for my boyfriend was so much easier, but I was willing to take a chance on this man whom I so enjoyed being with.

Me? A Full-Time Job?

When I got off of Social Security Disability I got on my knees and prayed to the only One who had an answer to what I was to do next. After all, I truly needed an income. I distinctly heard the name *Marlene* in that still small voice that Jesus shares. I knew who He meant and called Marlene the next day. Marlene Rider had recently begun her own business called Marlene's Home Care located in Cortland. I knew that she was looking for someone to work in the office as the Client Care Coordinator which meant that I would make the schedule for the caregivers to go to the homes of the elderly and take care of them. Some of the elderly needed 24 hour care so that meant three shifts to fill. It took a while to understand my job duties since I had never worked in this type of environment before. Marlene was very patient with me and in time, I began to understand what my duties were and then was given even more responsibility, such as interviewing and hiring employees. I enjoyed interviewing the caregivers and oftentimes questioned to see if they were Christians or not. The reason was that we wanted quality people who would not steal from the elderly and would hopefully have a good work ethic. As it turned out, if a caregiver did not show up at an elderly person's home for whatever reason, I would have to go there myself. I was not much of a medical person, so it would be fine if I just had to give a woman or a man a bath or take their blood pressure, but changing adult diapers and assisting in other ways was very hard for me to grasp. Although I had to do some of these duties, it definitely did not come naturally to me.

When I got the job at Marlene's Home Care, my hours were 8:00 AM – 5:00 PM with an hour for lunch.

I loved my job, but the best part about it was lunchtime. Actually, what I looked forward to was getting a phone call that said "It's almost Christmas!" With that, I would look out of the window and see Gary pulling up in his car, and I would be filled with joy just to spend an hour with him for lunch. Sometimes we would go to my trailer and eat, other times we would do fast food, but our favorite place to go was to Brother's Pizza in Cortland. I soon learned the love of Italian food that Gary had inherited from his Italian roots. I never met anyone in my life who loved pizza as much as Gary. He knew what kind of pizza dough and sauce each and every pizza shop had and beyond. He was not a "traditional" pizza connoisseur; "red with pepperoni" was just the tip of the iceberg. Gary introduced me to "gourmet" pizza, like chicken with ranch dressing, bacon and, of course, lots and lots of cheese. Although Gary was not overweight, his favorite topic was food, food, and more food. I got such a kick out of him, and I thought it was really funny that when he could not remember a word he would just make one up. I laughed and laughed when he would make up words because he couldn't think of them. Gary and I had so much fun together no matter where we went or what we were doing. It seemed that we did not go a single day without seeing each other for three years!

I was falling in love with a man who, unfortunately, was not in the least in love with me. This was so profound because I was so used to the same old guys from my past who would woo me with words, as my ex-husband had, as well as many others, giving me the line about how beautiful I was or how he was truly "falling in love," when it was just empty words. No, Gary was totally different. He was a hard catch who did not play games. I was experiencing what my prayer friends had talked about, which was becoming best friends with a man before marrying him or having sex. I guess they call it platonic. It was hard to remain abstinent, but God and Pastor Myron helped us remain pure. The physical attraction was overwhelming at times, but it was much more important for us to stay pure in the eyes of God as well as others, for that matter. I can swear to tell the hilarious truth that while all of this was going on, I never noticed in all the time that we dated how short Gary was. I mean SHORT! It wasn't until we did walk down the aisle in Holy Matrimony and I was wearing the flattest heeled shoes that I could find, did I take notice of how short Gary was. I never had really dated a short man and thought it funny that I was kind of blind to this fact.

When I would say "I love you." to Gary, instead of saying "I love you," back, he would say one of two things: either, "I laa laa you." OR "I'm not being fair to you." This would really get to me, but it also was extremely interesting to me. I had never ever dated a man who refused to even pretend to love me! It really made Gary mysterious. What the heck was going on in his mind? He obviously wanted to be with me day after day, and we spent a ton of time together, but he didn't love me…and admitted it. This was getting frustrating. Not only that, he never ever told me I was pretty. It was always the same line: "It must be the light." When Gary said "It must be the light," then I knew that for one instant Gary thought I was good-looking. Otherwise, there were no long stare downs full of lust; there was no arguing about spending the night with each other, there was truly no love for me on Gary's end of it. It was beginning to get to the point where I was asking myself what I was doing wasting my time with a man who would never commit to me, never want to marry me, or even fall in love with me, for that matter!

We did have one connection. Faith. Gary loved the Lord with all of his heart, as did I. We had a great time talking about our faith and the Bible and began going to each other's church. Gary soon became a member of North-Mar Church to make it official.

There were times when I would look at him and wonder… what was he thinking when he put that outfit on? It didn't match! I was a little embarrassed about the way he dressed to be honest, but soon found out what the problem was. Gary was color blind, as were his mother and one of his brothers. That explained why he never told me I had pretty blue eyes. He had no idea what color they were! Okay, so I could cut him some slack for that, I guessed.

Gary had also been speaking in tongues since about the same time years ago that I had, and so we began speaking in tongues together whenever we got the chance. There was and is so much power that is poured out when a person speaks in a heavenly language. God understands it, we don't. So after speaking in tongues we would get very quiet and listen to what God wanted to let us know though what is called "interpretation of tongues." As I spent more and more time with Gary, since we were speaking in tongues, I began experiencing the gift of discernment of spirits and the gift of the word of knowledge, and I became stronger as a Christian. I knew when something was of God; I would "know" it in my heart of hearts. The gift of discernment came right away and that meant I could walk through a busy store, like Wal-Mart, and just by looking in people's eyes, I could tell if they believed in Jesus or not. Some of the "or not's" were filled with such darkness, I struggled against looking in their eyes because what I saw was suffering, or worse.

What people do not understand, as it took me so long to understand, is that there is so much hope and so much love within a person who has the Holy Spirit living inside of them. In the book of Acts it explains that after Jesus had died on the cross and had been resurrected back to life three days later, He told His disciples that He had to go back to heaven, but He would leave them with something very powerful, and that was the Holy Spirit. So when you accept Christ as your Savior you are also inviting the Holy Spirit to come live inside you. It is all so supernatural and so fascinating that I can't even explain it well with words. All I know is I have come to understand a freedom, a being set free from all negativities!

God is the Father of lights and the Lord of LOVE! There are people who could be so much more in life if they were set free from all the nasty things in this world. Just walking through a store, I could see in people's eyes that he/she may be addicted to pornography, or were an alcoholic, or had a medical problem with their leg. Sometimes I was able to see people's sicknesses and diseases. The word of knowledge is a powerful gift and if not used correctly can truly cause problems. That is when I would have to ask God to show me when to keep my mouth shut and when to speak. Now THAT took a long time to figure out! I knew that speaking in tongues directly correlated to these different gifts of the Spirit, but I was not sure what to do with this knowledge or wisdom from the Lord, so to speak. So, I decided that whenever or wherever I was, when the Lord showed me that someone was a Christian, I would tell them. I would go up to strangers and say "God bless you, I see that you are a believer." The person would invariably smile and say "How did you know?" I would smile and say, "I could see Him shining through your eyes or spirit." This was the biggest compliment anyone who knows the Lord could ever get, and I was very confident in telling the person because it always came from God and not myself. Therefore it was always right on! God never makes a mistake!

Other times I did not know what to do with certain words of knowledge so I would just keep quiet. The Lord would show me that someone was addicted to drugs, or someone had a stomach ailment, or someone had been in jail or prison. In 2004, when I went to Cleveland and volunteered to work for three days for a Joyce Meyer conference, the word of knowledge was so strong after leaving the conference I decided to share what I saw with people. As I walked toward the parking lot attendant I looked at him with like an x-ray vision. I said "Hi, how are you doing today?" He said "Fine." And I said, "Let me ask you something, sir. When you were a little boy, did something bad happen to your mother?" He looked surprised and answered, "Yes, she was shot." I then told him other parts of his life, including a time he had spent in prison. This man wanted to know how I knew these things and so I told him. "The Lord showed me, but everything is going to work out in your life now since you've accepted Jesus and are walking along the straight and narrow." He was very happy that I spoke up. You see, a word of knowledge is always to encourage someone.

If I could see that maybe a marriage was splitting up, I would say a few words to encourage the person in staying with their partner, even without letting them know that I knew anything. I learned in time when to speak, when to write, and/or when to bring up what is going on in a person's life. Sometimes I would pray and pray until

God would show me who needed money or love, or whatever it may be, and God was always right on with the answer. God is so awesome, and He can be as big or as little in your life as you wish; it all depends on the person. I had been reaching for everything God had to offer me and it showed. I had never felt so stable, so loved and so filled with joy. I had experienced God's healing with the MS. I often would look back at all God had done for me and sit in a state of bliss, just resting in the Lord. He makes all things good, so bad news—especially of the medical kind—does not scare me any longer. My total trust and faith are in Him.

Conrad

Suddenly everything changed and all kinds of questions began to surface. One day in July of the year 2000 I had come back from lunch and was sitting at my desk reading over my schedule book when I heard loud footsteps running up the stairs toward my office. All of the sudden it seemed from out of nowhere, there he was, this huge hulk of a man standing right in front of my desk. When I asked how I could help him he replied that his parents had been taken care of by Marlene's Home Care a while back and they both had passed away, and he just wanted to talk to someone. Things really got "fishy" when Marlene saw him there, said "Hello" and this man, whose name was Conrad, nodded his head and then proceeded to sit down in my office chair and try to woo me into going out with him! This seemed so crazy! I was confused; especially since my boss, Marlene, acted as though it was just fine that this man spent the day with me—I mean ALL day—in my office listening to each phone conversation and asking me questions about myself. He asked if I was seeing someone and I told him the truth; that I was seeing someone but he was just my best friend, nothing more. I did not want to explain to this gentleman that although I loved him, Gary didn't love me and we hadn't made any commitment. It was awkward but yet it wasn't awkward, spending time with this man.

Conrad told me how much he loved Jesus and, of course, that was making him more and more attractive to me. He loved Jesus so much, in fact, that he played the part of Jesus in an Easter play every year at a local Tabernacle Church. He said they would put him on a cross with fake blood and he would hang there wearing nothing but a little cloth just like Jesus did. I was very impressed with his faith…and well, his looks…and, well, his uncommon interest in me.

Strangely enough, Conrad came back the next day and sat down and talked more with me. Realizing that my birthday was coming up soon he told me that he wanted to take me up in a hot air balloon ride with him for my birthday! I was shocked. Now how romantic was that! This Conrad was really amazing and he was so very interested in me, I did not know what to do. I thought about Gary. I didn't want to lose the wonderful friendship that we had together as he truly meant the world to me. But there, right in front of me, two days in a row, is this man who is built as they say, with six-pack abs, big muscular arms, tall and very handsome who genuinely wants to take me up in a hot air balloon. Not only that, he played the role of Jesus every year at Easter! I joked around and called him "Jesus." That was not good. Although I thought that I would be terrified up in a hot air balloon, with Conrad's strong arms around me, I knew I'd be just fine.

I explained to Conrad that I couldn't make any rash decisions because I had to be "fair" to Gary. I explained that I would need to speak with Gary about all of this, and had planned to, but I really didn't know how to bring it up. So, on my 37th Birthday, Gary and I were sitting on the couch in my trailer, laughing as my cat, Petunia, started intricately pulling the flowers out of the vase which Gary had bought me for my birthday. I was saying how appropriate it was for a cat named Petunia to be so interested in flowers. Right then, in the middle of our laughter, the phone rang. It was Conrad! I had not given my number out to him so he must have looked it up in the phone book. Anyway, Conrad was asking me, again, about going up in that hot air balloon while Gary was running around the trailer like a crazy man. He put his ear up to the phone and knew it was a man.

I was so uncomfortable, I was sure that I was showing my consternation about the situation to Gary, so I tried to get off of the phone quickly. When we hung up, Gary wanted to know everything about Conrad. I told him everything; about how he just "showed up" one day at work, about how he played Jesus at the Tabernacle on Easter, and about the hot air balloon ride that Conrad kept asking me about. I explained to Gary that he had never given me any kind of commitment or seemed to never want to marry me, let alone fall in love with me, so why couldn't I go out with Conrad? Gary was so upset he just left without saying good-bye.

That Wednesday night was torture, there was no choir practice so I went to a Bible Study and cried through most of it. Gary on the other hand was at another church that Wednesday night, feverishly praying on what to do about the situation. Both of us were really hurting emotionally. I was so confused that I kept calling Pastor Myron and Pastor Jim Garber for advice. Pastor Myron stated that it would be okay to go out with Conrad since Gary had not committed to anything, and Pastor Jim was saying things like, "This is not my department, I really don't know what to tell you. Have you called Myron?"

True Love from God

Finally…a call came through that very night. A miracle above all miracles and this is exactly how it transpired. I was wakened in the night around 2:45 AM to the phone ringing. I answered half asleep and heard Gary's voice on the other end. He seemed to be acting really weird. He first asked me, "Did you ever go out with that Jesus guy?" I responded "No." Gary kept telling me what a beautiful voice I had and how he loved to listen to me talk. He was really not acting like himself so I asked him if he was okay. He told me that he never felt better. He then said "I… I love you!" I was shocked. He loves me? Now? At 3 AM? Gary explained that God had filled him up to the top with a strong, passionate love for me. I began crying. There was absolutely no denial. There were no bribes, no loose false compliments, no sex craved man just looking for pleasure. This was it! Real! True! Love! It was God's pure love that was literally sent from heaven and deposited straight into the heart of my Gary. Wow! I was amazed. Gary said that the Lord kept telling him to call me and tell me about this love that God so freely poured into Gary's heart. This was truly unique…but I wanted to get back to sleep. We hung up only for the phone to ring again an hour and a half later.

"Nancy?"

"Yes, Gary?"

"May I come over?"

I was so tired but said, "Why not." Gary must have driven pretty fast as he got there sooner than I had anticipated. He walked into the room as I sat down and said, "I love you and I want to marry you."

This was the best thing that had ever happened to me. To be loved so purely without any alternative motives. To be loved by a man whose love came straight from God himself was the best love anyone could ever share. I called Pastor Myron and told him what

144

had transpired. Pastor Myron asked to see Gary and me right away in his office. He told us that we couldn't get married unless both of our ex's were married again. Thank God they both were. We never questioned why this was important but listened intently to Pastor Myron's wisdom. I knew the power of God that Pastor Myron had exhibited to me that had changed my life so profoundly. I knew that he would be the perfect person to give us pre-marital counseling. As Gary and I sat in his office it was soon apparent to both of us that we were <u>not</u> going to be getting married anytime soon if we were to put their trust in Pastor Myron and God. Myron stated that pre-marital counseling usually took about six weeks or less, depending on the couple. Gary and I agreed to the counsel, even if it did take six whole weeks. Now that we were engaged it would be even harder to stay pure, Pastor Myron told us, and he was right about that!

After six full weeks of marriage counseling, Gary and I were very excited that we would be able to make our wedding plans soon. The problem was that Pastor Myron told us that as God was his witness, we were not ready to be married. There was way too much baggage between us, and there needed to be some major healing in our hearts from past experiences with girlfriends and boyfriends and an ex-husband and an ex-wife. This was a very difficult time. Waiting and waiting and waiting, and trusting and trusting and trusting. Gary and I knew that we could trust God, but now it was time to trust this pastor with our lives because we wanted to be married right away!

Six long months later, (yes, I said six months!) Pastor Myron, Gary and I stood up together after our counseling session and Myron said loudly, "Okay, guys, this is it; you are ready to be married!" The three of us went into a bear hug and we never wanted to let go. Gary and I had grown to love and respect Pastor Myron and the feeling was mutual. We held on to each other as tears welled up, and Gary and I held on to each other and couldn't stop kissing. It was time to set the date. The date was tentatively already set for June 9, 2001. As Myron looked at his calendar, his facial expression changed as he said "I will be on vacation that week, so I can't marry you." I can't remember whose idea it was but we all agreed that Pastor Jim Garber would be the perfect man to marry us. We literally ran into his office and Myron announced that it was finally time for Gary and me to get married. We asked Pastor Jim Garber and he looked on his calendar and said yes, he could marry us. Gary and I were elated and I kept thanking God for bringing this man into my life who truly loved me with the love that God Himself deposited into him. It didn't matter how old we were, it didn't matter that Gary was short, it didn't matter where we decided to live, I knew that we were a perfect match. There was also always the anticipation of becoming one in the flesh, just like Jesus had wanted it to be for everyone from the beginning. I wanted to wear white as I was sure that I was a virgin again, and all the negativity of each and every man whom I had known before was gone—GONE in Jesus' name!

Chapter 16

The Speech that Changed my Life

While working for Marlene's Home Care I began getting phone calls from a woman named Rhonda Skinner who worked for a nonprofit business called Help Hotline Crisis Center, Inc. She had gotten my name and number from a gentleman from my church who also suffered from bipolar illness. Her job position was the Recovery Coordinator for the mentally ill, and she was proposing that I write a speech about my own recovery and share it at different organizations, such as Kiwanis clubs and Rotary Groups. I did, and received a $10 stipend for every speech that I made. In June of 2000, Rhonda had asked me to speak at a workshop located at a hotel and banquet center in front of hundreds of people. This was "the kick off" for the Recovery movement funded by a three year grant from the Ohio Department of Mental Health. When the day finally came for me to make this speech, my parents were present along with Pastor Myron and a good friend from church. Rhonda introduced me to three men that I remembered that day. She said that they were very important and I needed to do my best for them. One of them was named Ron Marian, the head of the Mahoning County Mental Health Board, another was John Myers from the Trumbull County Mental Health Board and, most important, was the Executive Director of Help Hotline Crisis Center, Inc. whose name was Duane Piccirilli. I stared at all three men when I shook their hands and tried to memorize what they looked like. After all, my future career was in their hands! Rhonda kept assuring me that one day I could become employed at Help Hotline and even take her job if she were promoted. She talked about the job as though it would be a lifetime change for me, and once I got hired I could assist all the mentally ill in the two county area—Trumbull and Mahoning. How? I did not know. I had practiced my speech on my personal recovery story and read it to anyone who would listen. Soon I had it down and felt confident that it was pretty good, mainly because my sisters said it was. I shared my speech at the Recovery workshop and did my best, although I was extremely nervous. There was another girl who also shared her story. She was a pioneer in our area to teach a course called BRIDGES. Prior to our speeches, a gentleman by the name of Tom Arens introduced us. As nice as he was, I was so nervous, I kept telling him to hurry up because I wanted to get it over with. Afterward he asked if there were any questions from the audience, and then he would give me the microphone to answer. He looked and acted just like a talk show host to me. It took me a long time after I was hired at Help Hotline to believe that Tom worked in mental health and was not hired out as someone who did this type of thing for a living. I got a pretty good overall reception from the evaluations that were filled out even though my mother stood up and announced, "Nancy, can always get jobs; she just can't keep them," which embarrassed me, but it was okay. There was another speaker whom I liked very much. She was the keynote speaker for the entire workshop and she had nothing but positive things to say about recovery from mental illness. I was beginning to think that there just might be hope for me.

In December of 2000 I finally had my job interview at Help Hotline with the Executive Director, Duane Piccirilli and Rhonda. I remember Duane asking me why I thought that I would be good for the job and I simply answered, "Because I have a passion to help people who have mental illness."

I started on my new journey with Help Hotline in December of 2000 saying "good-bye" to Marlene's Home Care. It was much more of a drive to get to Youngstown, but it was well worth it. I worked from 9 AM to 3 PM and got paid $4.00 more an hour than at Marlene's Home Care. It was a steady 32 hours-a-week job and I met some of the most wonderful people who worked at Help Hotline. I really mean that. Everyone was friendly and helpful.

One day I called my bank from Help Hotline to ask how much money was in my checking account, expecting the teller to tell me a number of around $500.00. I sat shocked when the woman said "$5,500.00." I said there must be some mistake, but no, it was definitely $5,500.00. I asked where the $5,000 had come from, and the response was, "The United States Treasury." I had been off of Social Security Disability for over three years, and they put $5,000 into my account. It didn't make sense at all! I called my sister, Chris, who was my advocate, and she, along with other family members, said, "Don't spend it." I did not spend it but made it my business to know why they gave me this money. I went to the Social Security office and explained it. I called the Social Security office in Baltimore, MD, and explained it. Then one day I received a letter in the mail stating that the Social Security office had made a mistake and it was their fault, and I was to keep the $5,000. It was amazing.

Over time I had read and understood that God is in charge of money. The Bible tells us to tithe 10% to the Lord, and some people have a problem with that, but the truth is—God doesn't need the money! It is all about us, not Him. Do we trust God with that 10%? Do we give with a cheerful heart, or do we give because we have to and then get angry about it? The truth is if you believe in Christ, you will realize that He owns the other 90% too! We are citizens of a kingdom that is literally "out of this world," and God will provide for those who trust Him with their money. I knew that this $5,000.00 was a gift from God. As I planned for our wedding I was well aware of the fact that if God wants a couple to be married, he will make the means available financially to do so. Knowing this confirmed even stronger the decision that it was God's will for Gary and me to marry.

Planning the wedding while working at Help Hotline turned into another job in itself. I felt the need to stay as stable minded as possible for my job but at the same time was ordering everything for my wedding. It was hard for me to separate the two. I even went as far as bringing my wedding dress to work as I was to get it hemmed right after work and had no time to drive all the way home. Thank God the management at Help Hotline was so very understanding!

Help from Above

Soon after we were married Gary and I started going to his old church for a while and I got to know some ladies who attended a Bible Study held at the home of a lovely woman named June Griffin. I was so absolutely blessed to become a part of this group which met weekly for a study in the spring and one in the fall. These ladies were mostly retired or semi-retired, or were homemakers, and I was always one of the youngest ones there, if not the youngest.

There was something so absolutely special about being in June's immaculate Holy Spirit-filled home. There was so much love and light and joy that filled that house. June Griffin was and is a woman of excellence. She is a person who wears a different beautiful knee length dress and high heels each and every day as she dresses up for Jesus. June is a woman of prayer. She has prayed for me when I was depressed and the depression just lifted totally out of my soul. One time she even prayed mania out of me, and all this over the phone! She called the mania "a familiar spirit." I had just returned from Pittsburgh where I had gone to a two-day conference for schizophrenia with a woman who claimed to be a Buddhist. When I returned home I desperately needed prayer, I called June and she prayed wholeheartedly over the phone and as she prayed, I felt the "familiar spirit" of mania lift off of me and the peace from God filling me up once again.

June has been instrumental in my life as an encourager and prayer warrior. One of the most interesting things about June is that although she knows nothing about mental illness, she can pray it away. She has an ability to talk to God and hear back from Him like no other woman I know. The truth is that June is a prayer warrior for a lot of people. Whenever I need prayer, I know to call June, and whatever the problem is, the issue is always lifted. I have sat in June's living room as we held hands and prayed, and I could see in the spirit what a large strong soldier of an angel June has standing behind her.

Our Bible studies are books for which June's daughter wrote study guides to go with them just for our group, not for publication. We have studied "The Battlefield of the Mind" by Joyce Meyer, "Blessed Beyond Measure" by Gloria Copeland, "Winning in Troubled Times" by Creflo Dollar, "Faith and Confession" by Charles Capps, "Transform Your Thinking, Transform Your Life" by Dr. Bill Winston, just to name a few. We would sit at June's dining room table and go around and share each answer to the questions from the workbook, and then we would go into prayer. We always prayed for the government and the President, his cabinet, and all the way down to our local officials. June is getting older in years, but nothing ever deters her from being a strong faithful woman of God. Her husband has done very well with his own business, and June has always been very generous to all who may have a need. My real desire is to become a strong prayer warrior as June is. I have noticed that if I ever go over to her house without calling first, I will find June sitting on her couch doing her own personal Bible study. She is a woman of integrity and a woman of her word. I would love to be like June Griffin "when I grow up."

Chapter 17

Gary's Brother Commits Suicide

We had only been married about six months when we received a late night call from Gary's mother, Dorothy and father Frank. She told us that she thought that Gary's brother, Jamie (Frank) had shot himself. In a state of utter shock and horror, we immediately got dressed and drove over to Jamie's house. As we walked into the house there was such a darkness and heaviness in the air as though Satan himself had permeated the rooms with his demons. The atmosphere was so thick with negativity that it was honestly difficult to walk. Jamie was in the bedroom and he had shot himself in the head. Dorothy was hysterical and Frank was in shock, but Gary felt the need—like his mother—to go into the room and see the horrible sight. I refused to look. Then Gary, Frank, Dorothy and I were invited by the neighbors to their home, right there in the middle of the night. The neighbor was a pastor and his son ushered us into their living room where we all sat around in disbelief. It seemed strange that they didn't mind being in their pajamas in front of us, but what really amazed me was how they opened their home to us. The pastor said that he had heard the shot fired at 10 PM, and he had a bad feeling that it may have been Jamie. Jamie was the nickname that his family called him. Jamie (Frank) Montagna was 16 years older than Gary. He had lived through the horrors of Vietnam, and all of his war buddies came rumbling in on their motorcycles to the funeral on that snowy December day. After the family and friends paid their respects, this large group of men, many wearing long white beards just as Jamie had, filled the room and asked ever so politely if they could do a "brotherly service" to the man they affectionately called "sick Sam". It was apparent that they loved him very much as each one spoke of their affiliation with Jamie.

Deep down, I was thinking how uncanny it was that all my life I had to fight off depression and suicidal thoughts, but here a new member of my "family" decided to truly end it all that way. Jamie was 54 years old at the time of his death, but he looked and talked like a man older than his own father. He had been through a lot.

Jamie did leave a suicide note. Unfortunately, it rambled on and on and was impossible to read which gave us the impression that he had drank or taken some other drug prior to pulling the trigger.

It was dreadful for Dorothy and Frank but I believe they came to terms with it better than anyone may have thought. They had seen Jamie suffer for years, not only with depression and posttraumatic stress disorder from the war, but also extreme pain from a back injury and other health issues. They were helping him in any way they could and actually were supposed to take him to a doctors' appointment the day before he passed away but Jamie could not go as he was feeling so bad. They had no regrets; they had done everything they knew how. Gary loved his brother very much but the age and lifestyle differences made it hard to become real close to Jamie. We used to call him on the phone just to listen to his hilarious answering machine message which basically said "Leave me alone!" in a gruff voice.

Years later, Dorothy and Frank got a call from one of the Vietnam vets who had Jamie's ashes and the group was planning to pour his ashes somewhere. They were very polite and respectful to Jamie's parents, but Dorothy and Frank decided they did not want to be a part of this ceremony.

Gary also has another brother who is twelve years older than he, and a sister who lives in South Bend, Indiana, who is five years older.

153

Each year Help Hotline hosts a SOS (Survivors of Suicide) walk in May and also a candlelight vigil in November in remembrance of family members who have lost a loved one to suicide. Some people have a photo of their loved one on a t-shirt which they wear for the walk. My present supervisor, Cathy, does a great job coordinating the two events along with the "members" of the two support groups that meet for condolence for their grief. Family and friends who are left behind after a person passes away go through grief but when it is a suicide there are so many unanswered questions and guilt along with a host of other emotions because of the act of suicide.

Help Hotline Position

At first I wasn't really sure what my role was at Help Hotline. Rhonda treated me as though I had a lot to offer as far as being "recovered" enough from the bipolar disorder, but in another way she made me feel that she needed to take care of me too. Rhonda had launched a new program (which I already mentioned) called BRIDGES (Building Recovery of Individual Dreams through Education and Support), and had three people teaching it in Youngstown. In order to teach BRIDGES, a person needed to have dealt with a mental illness. We were also supposed to attend a full week- long training in Dayton, Ohio, on how to teach the class through an organization called OAMH (Ohio Advocates for Mental Health). Before I could go to the training in Dayton, Rhonda asked me to help teach a class in Trumbull County. I enjoyed teaching my first class at a church in Warren along with two other teachers. I just went along and did what I was told to do—which was to read the class facilitator notes to the students. The class at the time was 15 weeks long and had some boring parts in it, (at least that is what *I* thought.) I was hoping to learn more and also how to make the class more interesting when I went to Dayton for the week long training.

At the training sessions I made many friends, including a lifelong friendship with the woman who was in charge of the BRIDGES Courses in Ohio who worked at OAMH (Ohio

154

Advocates for Mental Health). I enjoyed going to Columbus a few times a year to meet with the other BRIDGES teachers while staying at a hotel for the OAMH conference. It was interesting to meet all these people living here in Ohio who were also dealing with mental illness. There was a lot to do and many interesting workshops to attend.

I was asked by OAMH to be a presenter of the BRIDGES class in a workshop. People who had never heard of BRIDGES came into the classroom and I explained how it was taught, why it was taught, and how important it was that they begin teaching it in their area.

I also was asked to attend a two-week peer training and to teach the BRIDGES part of it with another woman whom I had just met when we got there. She and I taught the entire 15 week course in a condensed version in three days. It was a really difficult assignment! I actually did that part of the training two years in a row and OAMH paid me $250.00 each time.

At another type of conference I was asked to speak on: "Working and the Mentally Ill." I wrote a very comical speech about some of my experiences while working. One of the most ironic moments I had was getting a call from a temporary secretarial agency to work just one day at St. Joseph Riverside Hospital at the front desk of the Human Resources department. I had just been discharged from the psychiatric ward from the same hospital just the day before! As I sat at this big desk in my skirt and high heels, a nurse from the psych ward walked in. She looked at me with confusion and slowly started stammering "N-N-N-Nan...cy? Are...you...sure you are supposed to ...be up here?" I was so embarrassed because one of the other employees was my neighbor, and I didn't want her to find out that I had just had a *very* recent stay in the psychiatric ward. I whispered to Nurse Susan, "No, yes, wait....um, yes; I am working here just for today, honestly." After she did what she had come up there to do, I was sure she ran to the elevator to go back into the psychiatric ward to check my chart and make sure I had been discharged!

After I finished this speech, Dr. Fred Frese from Hudson, who has a PhD in psychology and had become a very well-known speaker himself, came up to me and said that he would like to make a speech with me someday. Having had his own struggle with mental illness, this meant the world to me. More people and organizations then began asking me to speak for different groups in the area, and I became known as an "over comer."

Quitting and Returning to Work

On July 13, 2001, I decided to quit my job at Help Hotline Crisis Center, Inc. having only been there eight months. Gary was working then and I was having some difficulty dealing with the MS returning because of the tanning booth. Old habits are hard to break, and one of my worst habits was to quit jobs without thinking twice. This time, though, I did not have Social Security to fall back on.

During the months that followed, I did absolutely nothing. I would get up and spend the morning with Gary, but when he left for work around 2 PM, I would lie on the couch without any TV or noise and just veg out until I went to bed. I did not know how to get out of my old habits. I wasn't really in a depression, but I was so upset about the MS I just stayed on the couch and vegetated. Taking lithium made me continually thirsty. I had had a strong addiction to Diet Coke for many years, drinking 2 two-liter bottles a day, and that—when all was said and done—did not quench my thirst at all. In 1998 when I was diagnosed with MS, I quit the Diet Coke habit altogether and began drinking water... water by the gallons. I had brought a frozen gallon jug of water to work every day and would chug it all down during the six hour work day. The dry mouth and excessive thirst was a really uncomfortable problem, not to mention the Diet Coke habit assisted many dentists to get rich. I had to have bonding on my front two teeth as well as many fillings over the years. While in Colorado I had had a tooth pulled for no real reason, but I did gain access to painkillers for the first time. "No reason," meaning I had had a toothache but waited out the 90 days to have my medical insurance kick in. By that time the tooth didn't hurt, but I wanted it pulled anyway. It was just the tip of the iceberg when it came to getting teeth pulled and going through horror because of it.

I really wasn't hopeful about what my future held when one day I received a phone call from Rhonda asking me if I would consider returning to Help Hotline. Rhonda said that the girl they had hired to take my place had just left, and would I be willing to return for ten hours a week. I was thrilled. I couldn't wait to see all the lovely people at Help Hotline again, and thankful that they were giving me another chance. I was interviewed again by Duane Piccirilli but don't remember if Rhonda was there during the interview or not. The first time I had worked for Help Hotline I was given the opportunity to be on the news and talk a little bit about the recovery of mental illness. Being naïve and not knowing what to say, I told the entire viewing audience that Jesus Christ and reading the Bible is the best way to recover from mental illness. Although I still believe that to this day, it wasn't appropriate when representing Help Hotline. Even with my mistakes Duane hired me back and I was thrilled with the chance to work only ten hours a week!

Help Hotline, a nonprofit organization that has thrived over the years, is one of the most interesting places to work. The success of Help Hotline is mainly due to the leadership of Duane Piccirilli, the CEO, and Cathy Grizinski, the Associate Executive Director. Duane has a way with funders and grants. The three-year grant from the Ohio Department of Mental Health for the Recovery program ended, but Duane made it his business to keep the Recovery Program going. He asked for the two local boards to assist along with a grant committee in Cleveland. I was soon given more hours at Help Hotline and was up to 25 hours a week. This worked out well for me and I loved the job. Where else could a person get hired for HAVING a mental illness? I had tried to hide my illness from employers for years, and now it was the reason I was hired. Who could think of a better fit for a job?

I liked the job so much that I didn't mind the long half-hour drive to get there. One morning while driving to work, everything seemed like it was going smoothly, as far as my car was concerned. I parked in the parking lot and went inside the building. Suddenly the bookkeeper announced that she smelled something burning. One of the other employees went outside and discovered my car engine was on fire! Duane made everyone evacuate the parking lot as they called 911. The fire truck arrived and turned the water hose on my engine, and then my car was towed away. There I sat at the conference room table wondering what in the world I was going to do as I called Gary and told him what had happened. The very next day my parents loaned me another car that eventually became my own. I was thankful to be alive because the fire had not started until I was actually parked in the parking lot. The Lord was once again protecting me and keeping me safe from harm. Praise be to God!

Working at Help Hotline gave me many opportunities to help others with mental illness. The courses that are taught are called BRIDGES (Building Recovery of Individual Dreams through Education and Support) and WRAP (Wellness Recovery Action Plan).

The reason that I enjoyed my job so much was because I was helping the one group of people whom I loved the most, the mentally ill. No one can understand how painful living with a mental illness is unless they have experienced it themselves.

I had no idea what my future held when I made the commitment to go back to my job at Help Hotline but somehow I knew my life could only get better if I stuck with it...and I was right about that! Rhonda had moved on to another job and Cathy Grizinski became my supervisor and still is to this day. Her dedication to Help Hotline assists me with my own dedication to the cause of the company. She also treats me very well and has helped me out and taught me so much - more than anyone would ever know.

Chapter 18

Buying a House!

My husband, Gary, holds an Engineering degree from Youngstown State University. He has worked as a consulting engineer at several plants, sometimes as far away as Cleveland. All Gary wanted was a steady job that was close by that paid well. He found that at a local plant, and while working there we saved up enough money to move out of my trailer and into a real home.

I used to pray on my knees about our finances. Well, one particular morning, I got my answer. God told me that I need not ever pray about our finances again. He explicitly let me know that He would personally take care of us financially. I have had peace about this ever since. The other interesting thing is, it was great for our marriage for me to understand that God is not limited by our jobs or our paychecks because He owns it ALL! He can do anything with our finances to make them work out if we just trust Him instead of a job. God is so good. He brings peace if we just ask. God has brought a lot of peace to our marriage because we stand on His promises, not the world's ideas.

That said, in 2004 we started a hunt to find a house to move into. Gary was adamant that he no longer wanted to live in the tiny trailer park in Cortland. We went through a realtor company that we liked and looked at house after house after house. Finally, on my birthday, we walked into a certain house in Warren, and I knew that we really needed to bid on this house; it was definitely where we were supposed to live. I told Gary and the realtors that this was the house for us! After talking it over with my parents, my father didn't think it was a good idea to move and wanted us to stay in the trailer. Gary's parents said the exact opposite. They said, "Bid lower, because the house isn't worth as much as they are asking." Well, we did bid low and someone else got the house at one point. As it turned out, there had been two different families who had made a bid on this house, but neither one of them had the financial backing to purchase it. We were so absolutely blessed to find a lovely competent lady assist us with our banking loan and get us a fixed rate of 4.99 % interest. In 2005 we moved to our house and have thoroughly enjoyed living in this home ever since. As I said, God has always been so good to us financially. We moved in November right before Thanksgiving, and we had our family over for Thanksgiving dinner at our new home, which was wonderful.

Another Diagnosis?

While working at Help Hotline I had an appointment a psychiatrist that I had known for many years, Dr. Praseed, who unexpectedly told me I needed to go to The Nephrology Group and have my kidney function checked. I had been on Lithium for so long that the doctor thought it would be a good idea. (Lithium, being a salt, can damage the kidneys) I did as he asked and went to see Dr. Sojourn, the Nephrologist. I didn't think much about it until I received a phone call from Dr. Sojourn asking me to make another appointment to return and have some more tests done. I told Dr. Praseed and he said something to the effect of "maybe they just want your money." I just laughed but knew that there might be a chance that my kidneys weren't up to par. Meanwhile, Dr. Sojourn had moved away and my new doctor was Dr. Nahum. He gave me a report the next time I saw him that there clearly was kidney damage, although he did not tell me how bad, and started me on medication.

Dr. Nahum was questioning whether I should be taken off of Lithium. One day I called The Nephrology Group and talked to Dr. Nahum's nurse about my medication. The nurse told me then that my kidneys were only working 50%. When I asked why the doctor hadn't told me this, she replied, "Well, it isn't easy to tell someone that their kidneys are only working 50%." I was upset that the doctor hadn't told me this when he saw me. Again, I felt the stigma of having a mental illness was the reason they hadn't mentioned this information to me. When someone is deemed Bipolar, other people are afraid of "upsetting them." I believed this to be true in my case. I was put on high blood pressure medication and a water pill since I had been experiencing edema with swollen ankles. It took a long time to get the medicine regulated correctly, and in time, I was also prescribed an iron pill to counteract anemia. I went along with the entire regimen that The Nephrology Group prescribed for me.

My psychiatrist was quite concerned and told me that if he had not seen me in 1994 (the last time I had been hospitalized) in that overly manic state, he would have taken me off of Lithium right away. However, I had remained stable for 12 years and didn't think getting off of Lithium would be a problem and was not afraid to try it. In 2006, Dr. Praseed finally gave the go ahead to get off the Lithium, and, at my request, to get off of the Klonipin also. I followed the plan of my psychiatrist and slowly went off both medications. It was not long until I felt I was in big trouble. I was experiencing major anxiety and depression. I was experiencing panic and fear like I never had before. All the women in my Bible study prayed for me to take the fear away but it seemed like nothing worked. I was quoting scripture every day, all day, and trying to believe in a healing process, but the nightmare kept recurring and the fear was overwhelming every minute of every day. I was planning to go to a 4th of July party in 2006 and I just couldn't make a decision to go or not. I kept calling my mother saying I was going one minute and then calling her back the next to say I wasn't. The following day, I chose to go to the psychiatric ward. Gary was not used to this kind of behavior and he allowed me to drive to the hospital by myself and suffer it out in the ER. I was given the usual shot of Ativan, but it didn't even touch my anxiety. And I did not feel any better when I was admitted to the psych ward. In fact, I felt worse. A Dr. Kane, a different nephrologist from The Nephrology Group, came to see me every day which only reminded me that I had kidney disease and brought more fear upon me. The worst part about it was that my psychiatrist had ordered a test where I had to urinate in this special cup that was on ice and had to remain on ice every day. It was then *my* responsibility to make sure that the nurses kept this crazy contraption on ice which only added to my anxiety. Finally, when the test was over, Dr. Praseed, the psychiatrist told me that my kidneys were only working 37%. He then proceeded to increase my anxiety by telling me that I would probably last eight years on dialysis. I asked Dr. Kane about this and he said, "Your psychiatrist is not a nephrologist, so he doesn't know what the future holds for your kidneys." But I chose to believe Dr. Praseed and think the worst with a bundle of anxiety.

I stayed in the Psych Ward for four days but never felt any better. The doctor was trying all kinds of new combinations of medications on me, but nothing seemed to work. I went back on Klonipin, though nothing seemed to stabilize my mind. In time, however, I did begin feeling better, but, although I had lived it all before, I was not prepared for the acute mania that lay dead ahead.

At the end of February of 2007 the excitement of mania started brewing once again. I had met the CEO of channel 45/49 and had a great conversation with her at a workshop for work. We became e-mail buddies. I was sure that there would be a documentary about my life and the lives of others. This isn't just being overconfident and proud. It's mainly just the effect of the illness. At the time I was thriving at work, and in March 2007 I set up training for ten mental health consumers to become WRAP facilitators. During this period I was really manic, and when it came time for the training, the Ohio "master trainers" were getting a little bit uncomfortable with me. When it was my turn, I was chosen to teach the part on changing negative thoughts to positive thoughts. I knew that using the living words of scripture is the only way to really help a person feel better, but when I read the scriptures, that made one of the master trainers so uncomfortable he yelled, "No religion in the WRAP class!"

The other event taking place in my life was that I was asked to write up a testimony for church at the Easter Contata. Gary and I were back at North-Mar church and I was, again, a part of the choir. I wrote my testimony and shared it with Pastor Jim Garber, who, in turn, told me that it was good. I also kept listening to the practice CD and felt compelled to practice the solo that went along with the testimony. The song was called "Faithful," and I practiced it day and night. When I asked Jim if I could try out for the song, he said something to the effect of "Don't be disappointed if I don't let you sing it." I stated that that was fine, and then one day I sang the song for Jim and he said it was "beautiful." I practiced and practiced this song until I thought I had it down pretty well. Then came the test. During a choir practice when Jim asked me to come up and sing the song, I was so nervous about singing it in front of everyone that my heart was pounding out of my chest. After that, at another choir practice, I read my testimony to the choir. Some of the people were actually crying and others were in shock, not knowing all that I had gone through in my life.

I was getting more manic as the days rolled on. I started to become obnoxious at work, which really made it difficult for my supervisor and the CEO. I would storm into the CEO's office and tell him all sorts of things that were going on. I really drove him crazy. I began a new side career selling Arbonne which was a company that sold wellness products and telling everyone that they needed to use it. I even gave samples to Duane who used the product when he shaved and agreed with me that it really worked well. I didn't get too far with this job…and all of this was very embarrassing for me afterward.

The twin sister of a woman who used to work at Help Hotline passed away, and some of the folks from the Crisis Center went to her calling hours. That particular morning I had burnt my wrist on my clothes dryer, and as I sat in the pew of the church listening to the "Celebration of Life," I kept looking at my wrist and noticed that it was getting better and better…or so I thought. I was sitting there in quite a delusion. There were so many false thoughts and weird ideas running through my mind because I was truly going into psychosis. I saw Dr. Praseed once a week during this time and he kept me out of the hospital, although he kept telling me that I was basically on the brink of madness. I was probably not hospitalized because my doctor knew that I had committed to do this testimony and solo at Easter time, and if I went into the psych ward, I wouldn't be able to do it.

At work my supervisor asked me if I could have all the mental health consumers at the Community Center make cards for the volunteers who answered the phones at the crisis line. I took this opportunity to have a type of "card making party" at the group homes as well as the Community Center. My manic zeal made all of the mental health consumers as excited as I was about making the cards, and some of them made two or three cards each. It was a lot of fun for me, and when I showed Dr. Praseed the cards that had been made, he remarked that my mood was "infectious." It was kind of the story of my life; people just loved to be around a happy person, but the moment the deep depression hits, that's when you find out who your real friends are. Even then, your *friends* don't always want to be around you. As the saying goes, it's the "Negative Nancy" syndrome. (no pun intended)

I also was having a problem with the television talking specifically to me, no matter what channel or program it was. Everything became one big **coincidence.** *This* meant *that* and *that* meant *this.* I was so overwhelmed with this post traumatic response to something that happened a long time ago that I was not able to think about anything else. It was the rape I had endured while living in Rhode Island. It was something that I had buried so deep that I truly was in denial that it had happened. But now, during this period of time, prior to sharing my testimony and song at church I could not get it out of my mind. I kept reliving it over and over and it was literally torturing me. It was obvious Satan did not want me to share this powerful testimony as he was doing everything to stop it.

A Lift from a Friend

In the meantime, I noticed a new employee named Esther who worked in the phone room. Esther was an African American who had a "presence" of God, like an anointing on her. I had never spoken to Esther before but was sure that she could help me. I approached Esther one day and told her the dilemma I was in. I had to do this testimony and solo, but all I could think about was this rape that had happened many years before. Esther took charge and asked me to go into my office. It was there that the power of God took over. Esther wrapped her arms around me and prayed, "People call this Posttraumatic Stress Disorder, but I call it the devil!" I held on to Esther for dear life as I felt a transformation coming on. It happened all at once. The demonic spirit that was oppressing me with a continual stream of flashbacks to this horrifying event just left me like a huge weight being lifted off of my heart and mind. I never thought of the rape again (until I mentioned it in this book and, again, had to fight off the PTSD – see Chapter 13). Well, the devil did not want me to give my testimony at the Easter Cantata, and that is why I was attacked so strongly not only with mania, but also with this PTSD. The Easter Cantata was on a Friday evening and a Sunday afternoon, and I had invited everyone to my house after the Cantata to celebrate. My friend Rhoda flew in from Phoenix for the event and helped me out immensely, along with my sister Linda from Maryland. The night finally came for the concert and I was so glad to actually do it, and hoped and prayed that afterward I would come out of this manic state. The Lord got a standing ovation after I sang my song Friday evening, and the same happened again Sunday afternoon, but by this time, I was acting pretty crazy filled with mania. As I mentioned in front of nearly 1,000 people each time how inappropriate my manic behavior had been in my lifetime, I was actually going through it again! I had written the testimony out in February and read it verbatim so there was no extra weird stuff added in. Thank God! Poor Gary was beside himself throughout this whole ordeal and tried to do his best to keep me calm. I was ranting that

Sunday afternoon and Gary was so upset with me that he didn't even go to the concert! He was also upset because I had planned another party at our house after the Sunday afternoon concert and Gary was really dead set against it. He was becoming well aware of how dramatic this mental illness had become and it kept raging on even after the concert. I worked fewer hours and was basically off work the whole week of the concert. They truly understood at work, (not that my supervisors liked it) but they tried to help me. I just had to ride this high wave that I was on... Okay, it was more like a tsunami!

I even made up a name for Gary's and my new musical group. It was a mix between gospel and rock music that Gary was so good at playing on his guitar, so I named it "Montagna Mental Health Mountain Music." Gary didn't like this name as he really was not a country fan at all, but he really dared not disagree with me no matter what I said or did. I was on a mission and nothing could stop me now! Even at the meetings at the local mental health board I would tell of my plans to teach each and every person at the community center to play an instrument. I took Gary to two music stores and proudly explained to the owners that I would be purchasing many instruments for the community center. I remember Gary saying when we got back to the car, "You didn't make any sense in there. What are you talking about...buying everything in the store....we can't afford to do that!" I informed him that the Crisis Center would be able to purchase all the instruments. God bless Gary!

During this period of time I was called upon at a meeting for work, and when asked if I had anything to tell about what was going on with the Recovery program, I announced that I was going to start teaching each person at the community center how to play an instrument. And in addition to that, my husband and I were going to be sharing mental health music for all the mentally ill to listen to and get help from. I went on in detail to the point where I had everyone in the room—all of these mental health professionals—smiling. I later told the CEO of the board that next time there was a meeting would he please put some duct tape over my mouth before I spoke!

I also shared with a few people that if I could put mania in a bottle, it would certainly make me a rich woman.

The problem is that when a person is manic, one does not recognize it in oneself, and I was really the last one to realize this. But then one day in order to prove that I was not manic, I made an appointment with a very well-known therapist at the local counseling center. This woman seemed happy to listen to me and all of my fabulous ideas. I was out to prove that I was going to become famous and that everything I had said at the meeting earlier was true and would come to pass. But as she sat there listening to me, she became quite uncomfortable, and I thought that she was uncomfortable for all the wrong reasons. She then asked me if I would like to go stay at a special place for people who were severely mentally ill, "…just for a break." I told her that I was appalled and said that my home was my sanctuary and I would not consider going anywhere for help. After I explained to her everything I had announced at the meeting that morning, the therapist called a gentleman who had been at the meeting into the room to confirm that what I said was inappropriate. He came in and greeted me, "Hi Nancy!" She then proceeded to ask him what I said in the meeting and that made me mad because I felt I was being cornered. But he replied, "Oh no, Nancy was okay at the morning meeting. She had stated that her husband plays a mean guitar and I understood, because I play the guitar, too." I smiled and said, "See, I am telling you the truth, there is nothing wrong with me."

She then asked me if I would like to come back, to which I replied, "No," and so she said that they would forget about the appointment and I would not have to pay for the visit. I was sure that this woman was all messed up and jealous of me for all the good things that had happened to me recently.

I shared with my friend, Dana, who also had bipolar illness, that I was going to become famous, she said "But you are already famous in the mental health world." I said, "No…I mean *worldwide.*" There was nothing Dana could say; I just would not take "No" for an answer. I said that I was going to publish a book, and Dana

167

suggested that the name of the book be called "Our World," because there are only those of us who are mentally ill that actually understand what it is like, a world that is so different from the average person's. Obviously, I did manage to publish a book but the name? Again, obvious.

Back then I felt that everyone understood mental illness because I had so many friends who suffered with it, not unlike me, but I have since learned that that wasn't true at all. Most people do have misconceptions about mental illness, along with the stigma and misunderstandings and all sorts of wrong ideas about those who suffer from it. "This is a real disorder with a real solution," I would say to people. Is anyone aware of how many people who are famous have had mental illness? I have a list of those who have admitted to depression and bipolar disorder. Even Abraham Lincoln suffered immensely with depression and mania. He had many failures before he became president, but the secret was that he never gave up. This is something that I tell my classes. Never give up, never give up, and never give up! It was actually Winston Churchill who was asked to make a speech at an Ivy Leaguer college graduation and he just repeated those three sentences. Winston Churchill, ironically, also suffered from depression and called it his "black dog." The list of famous people with depression goes on and on. Many are writers, poets, actors and songwriters. Jim Carey, Drew Carey, John Denver, Rodney Dangerfield, Jonathan Winters, Ellen Degeneres, Margot Kidder, Dick Cavett, and Billy Joel have all publically stated that they have had bouts with depression. It seems that those people with a creative brain may have the tendency to suffer the most with mental illness, but it can happen to anybody in any walk of life. I had met so many people who suffered from mental illness that I began realizing that it really was not a curse to live with this type of illness and that it could be a blessing, because it helps to empathize with other people with compassion and love.

Chapter 19

The Manic Depressive Support Group

Prior to working at the Crisis Center, I had been involved with a support group called "The Manic Depressive Support Group" which was formed long before the name was changed to Bipolar Disorder. (The new name for this support group is DBSA for Depression and Bipolar Support Alliance) I was friends with each and every person in the group and had a good time with all of them. There were regular elections of officers, and sometimes I would be elected Secretary, which meant that I would type up a newsletter and mail it out to everyone in the group. (Once the head nurse at St. Joes psych ward let me use her typewriter to get the newsletter out in time) I was also elected President of the support group, meaning that I needed to be at each meeting and be willing to facilitate. We even went so far as having a few "facilitator trainings" led by a professional who was a sort of overseer for the group.

Every week that the group met, there were people there who were seriously suicidal, and there were also a few who had completed suicide during those years or later.

One member of the group whose name was Kevin came every week, and every week he would state that he wanted to commit suicide. He was an obese man who suffered from Crones' disease which, we were told, could also cause depression. Kevin came one week and told us that he had been eating at KFC one Saturday night on the west side, which wasn't the best side of town. As he finished off his meal, he noticed a man coming in the door with a gun who went up to the counter, pointed the gun at the woman working there and demanded all the money in the register. Kevin suddenly had a great idea. Instead of committing suicide, he could politely ask this robber if he would please take him out of his misery and shoot him dead. Kevin got up from the table and awkwardly started running out the door after the man with the gun. He was yelling, "Come shoot me! I don't want to hurt you, I won't call the police, just please shoot me!" Kevin told the group this story and then said sadly that if he hadn't been so fat, maybe he could have caught up to the guy and the man would have shot him.

Kevin was so suicidal that he had actually contacted Dr. Kevorkian. Remember, Dr. Kevorkian was the man who used to assist people with suicide if they were in pain or at the end of their lives. He would be paid a fee to give the person a shot that would kill the person without any pain. Kevin pleaded with Dr. Kevorkian to assist him with his death, but because Kevin had no other life-threatening disease besides depression, he would not do it.

Kevin had applied for Social Security Disability and received a letter in the mail from the Social Security office stating that he would be awarded a lump sum retroactive from when he first applied, somewhere in the neighborhood of $10,000. Kevin came to the group that week and told us all about the money he would be receiving. He then started in with his usual sob story about how depressed he was and how much he wanted to commit suicide. One of the men in the group who was quite instrumental in keeping the group going and was somewhat a friend to Kevin took a new approach with Kevin. Instead of the usual encouragement not to commit suicide, this gentleman, Tom, stated "Well, Kevin, you finally will have the money to buy a gun, so maybe it is time for you to go ahead and commit suicide, since that is obviously what you want to do." All of us looked at Tom as though he had just lost his own mind. I began processing what Tom was saying and why, and decided to agree with Tom. I said "Yes, Kevin, you have been telling us how badly you want to die. Well, now you have the money to do it! You can afford to buy a gun." Kevin didn't say a word.

When Kevin actually did receive the check, he told us that he had always wanted to go to a baseball game in another state, but was never able to go because he did not have the money. Now he had planned this trip but needed a ride to the airport, and I told him I would take him there. I picked up Kevin at his house which he shared with his father and drove him to the airport, giving him a pep-talk all the way. I tried to reason with Kevin that God loved him and didn't want him to die. Kevin answered with some odd scripture that he stated was in the Bible about some people being put here on the earth only to suffer, and that he was one of those people. I was not sure about *that* scripture as I had never heard of such a thing. Meanwhile Kevin just droned on and on about how badly he wanted to commit suicide. It really was tiring after a while, to hear this constant negativity from him. Sadly, he wasn't close enough with anybody to take a trip like this with, and he was always going places alone. I was glad when I got Kevin to the airport so I could have a nice ride home listening and singing to music.

A few weeks had gone by when I got the phone call: "Kevin is dead." It was Tom. Tom and I assumed that he died of a self-inflicted gunshot wound to the head, but the obituary stated "natural causes." I waited patiently until I heard that the autopsy was completed, and then went over to Kevin's house to talk with his father about how Kevin died. When the man opened the door, I saw the worst case of hoarding that I had ever seen or ever will see again in my life. There was paper coming out of the front door! I saw an enormous collection of albums which Kevin had always talked about. I apologetically introduced myself and asked Mr. Ross if he could tell me if Kevin really died of natural causes or had committed suicide. Mr. Ross stated that Kevin had been sleeping and rolled out of his bed onto the floor and died of natural causes, not suicide. All of our group concluded that Kevin, at 40 years old, had prayed to die for so long that it seemed that God had just taken him.

The vice president of the support group had the responsibility for getting monthly speakers to come and talk to us about a subject concerning mental illness. The one in charge of this at the time, Randy, was also seeing Dr. Praseed back then, and I had persuaded him to come to the group to speak. I had informed him about other psychiatrists who had come to speak but only told us that these illnesses get worse over time, which made everybody feel horrible by the time they were through. Dr. Praseed was a good speaker but, unfortunately, he was not an advocate of having a support group like the one we had, mainly because of all of the "hook-ups'" between men and women who were mentally ill and normally would not "hook up" with each other. The group didn't quite understand what he meant, although we all knew that there was a lot of sex going on within the group, and that some—or maybe all—of it was quite inappropriate. In all actuality there was even a young girl who was underage who was having sex with a man who could have been her grandfather. This man also saw Dr. Praseed and had told him everything. There were a few of the people from the group that had a kind of orgy at his house, and Dr. Praseed spoke against it, rightfully so. He was trying to convey this to all of us, but several felt that those things that happened outside of the group were none of Dr. Praseed's business, and were mad at this man who had told him everything. I later believed that this was the only reason that Dr. Praseed, with his busy schedule, had agreed to speak that night, trying to let us know that outside of the night of the support group meeting, it would be a good idea not to get together in any other way, shape or form.

Murder

There was a young man in the group by the name of Mark who was very personable and handsome. He lived with his mother in a beautiful house in Struthers, Ohio. He had had a few parties in his basement apartment of this lovely home, and the group enjoyed going there. He was always a lot of fun during the meetings and afterward when we would go out to eat. He was liked by everyone, but one strange thing about him was that he never spoke about his own illness, almost as if he did not believe that he had an illness. He did, in fact, have a bad case of psychosis at one point and had told us that he was going to ride on the white horse like Christ and have a large part in the second coming of Christ. Because of that, it was decided that one of us needed to take Mark to the hospital and into the psych ward, and I volunteered to do it. I approached Mark very carefully and told him in order to prove that there was nothing wrong with him, I wanted to take him to the hospital to be evaluated. Surprisingly, Mark agreed to go, but we spent hours and hours at the hospital in this little tiny ER room waiting for someone to come from the local counseling center to evaluate him. Each time a doctor or nurse would come in the room Mark would become convincingly normal and state that he was not a "harm to himself or to others." (Which is now the criteria to be admitted) He'd then point at me and tell them that I was the one who was mentally ill. I would say, "No, it's Mark. He thinks he is coming back with Christ." But he would deny ever saying that.

When the pre-screener finally got there from the counseling center, Mark promised that he wouldn't point me out as the sick one, and he did answer all the questions as normally as he could. Again, he told the screener that he was not a "harm to himself or others". I was so mad. They actually let him go with no additional hospital time, and I had to drive him all the way back to Struthers. I did not get home until nearly 5 AM. All those hours at the ER were wasted, and I decided then and there that that was the last time I would go out on a limb trying to help someone as he was literally driving *me* crazy in the ER. Mark was obviously very much in need of help, but talked himself out of getting admitted to the psychiatric ward where he belonged.

Not long after that night, Mark moved to a trailer park and began a new life living on his own. One of the women from the support group also lived in that trailer park, and although Mark wasn't attending the meetings at the time, she had gone to visit him, and told us that he was doing some drugs and acting very bizarre. I realized after that long night at the ER that it didn't seem possible to try to get help for Mark again, because he was really good at masking his illness.

While I was working at Marlene's Home Care I had a phone call from a member of the support group. "Nancy," he said, "you need to buy a newspaper! Mark is on the front page." "What happened now?" I asked. "He killed a man!" was the response over the telephone. Wow, that was a shock! I quickly obtained a newspaper and read the details. Mark had actually murdered someone using a blunt object, and the evidence was everywhere, the police stated. He had given the police a statement that was something to the effect of the victim being a type of alien and he had no other choice but to kill him. Shock waves exploded through the support group and beyond. It seemed that every person I knew was talking about Mark. After all the time I had spent with him, it was hard for me to believe. I thought that he would have been the last person on earth to murder someone.

While Mark was awaiting his sentencing, his mother telephoned me, hoping that her son would be acquitted using the "By reason of insanity" plea. I, too, felt that had Mark not been mentally ill, he would have never committed this crime, and that he had a very good chance. Mark's mother then asked if I could go visit Mark in the jail and talk to him about it. I said I would go if one of the men from the support group would go with me.

Tom and I from the support group went to the local jail and asked for Mark. We waited there until Mark appeared fully dressed in his jail attire and looking as handsome and neat as he always had. Tom spoke to him first and asked how he was doing and made some small talk. When he was through, I took the phone. "Hey, Nan!" Mark exclaimed as nonchalantly as if he were just running into me at the local mall or something. I was very cautious with him. I took a deep breath, looked him in the eye and said, "Mark, I know you would never have done what you did had you not been mentally ill." Mark's reaction startled me. He stated "The man was a type of alien and it had to be done." I was at a loss for words. I was just trying to see where Mark was coming from, and hoping that he would realize that his mental illness had taken over when he committed this horrible crime. As I looked into his eyes, his demeanor changed suddenly and he said, "Hey, listen, Nan, I am in the middle of a card game, so I'm going to say 'good-bye' now." This didn't come as any big surprise since Mark was one who made friends quickly and knew how to fit in wherever he was. I was somewhat relieved to have the conversation end and looked up at Tom who nodded for me to hang up the phone. I said good-bye and reluctantly hung the phone up. As Mark hung up, he turned around, glanced back at Tom and me, and then waved at us with a bit of a smile on his face. He then walked out of the room through another door with a guard. I thought at that moment that all I could do was pray for him. As it turned out, he ended up on medication, and so was perfectly sane to stand trial. He received 17 years in prison for manslaughter.

Of all the people I knew who had mental illness, there were very few who ever talked about or tried to murder anyone else.

Chapter 20

Victims

I have met many people over the years who were suffering from mental illness. There have been hundreds who have taken the BRIDGES and later the WRAP classes. Each and every person who has taken the classes is special to me and I love them all.

The truth is that people with mental illness are more often victims themselves, especially those who are living in group homes. Many of them have no income except for a monthly check from Social Security Disability, and while some landlords are compassionate and helpful, there are others who will take full advantage of the situation, spending the person's money and treating them unfairly. There are some landlords who ridicule the people who live in these group homes and say unkind things just to hurt them to keep them in line, so to speak.

One person suffering from a mental illness can be extremely challenging for the whole family. I was always concerned that my three sisters may have been jealous or bitter about the fact that our father had been so generous to me financially and made sure that I always had a car to drive. But I found that was not the case, because my sisters had wanted to assist me too in any way that they could as they had watched me go through such difficult times. I was amazed later in life to know that two of my sisters actually had put me in their will along with their own children.

Over the years we had trained many BRIDGES teachers, and while some of them became very competent teachers, others either weren't ready to make the commitment to teach at least three courses, or they moved on to better things, which is what we liked to see. The confidence that is engendered from actually "giving back" to the mentally ill—and also getting paid—was great to watch! One teacher has gone on to become a supervisor with PATH Homeless Outreach and also takes care of the day-to-day operations at the Help Hotline Community Center. We teach the BRIDGES and WRAP classes there as well as at Trumbull Memorial Hospital. I was born in that hospital and have been in the psychiatric ward of that hospital, and now have taught many classes at that facility. We have had many touching validations from people saying how much the class helped them. Help Hotline has also received letters in the mail from students telling how their lives have been changed by the classes.

Teaching the courses in Youngstown has opened doors for people who are stuck in the vicious circle of using and abusing drugs and alcohol. They are assigned by the court to follow a two year program of staying clean, attending AA (Alcoholics Anonymous), NA (Narcotics Anonymous), and/or the BRIDGES and WRAP courses along with other mandatory groups and therapy. We as teachers have learned so much from them. Sometimes I get a call from a case manager who will tell me "Jimmy will be missing class next week because he is in jail." The person will be back the following week and I am amazed how a person can spend a week in jail and still come back to class with a smile. We often say "No Horror Stories" as a "comfort agreement" (rules) for the class, but once in a while the substance abuse stories are so interesting and foreign to us, we let them tell their story. One woman, Kate, had worked at Red Lobster for many years. During her shift as a waitress, she would excuse herself to the restroom, having brought all of her drug paraphernalia secretly in her purse, and "shoot up" heroin while in the bathroom stall. She would then resume her shift as a waitress and nobody knew otherwise!

One young gentleman in his 20's is known for being a walking, talking miracle. He had alcoholism so badly that his esophagus was that of a 70 year old man. He would drink two or more bottles of Vodka every day, throwing up and then drinking more. It had gotten way out of hand. His mother could not stand to see the withdrawal from alcohol that he endured when he ran out of it, so she enabled him by bringing bottles over to his apartment. He told me that he would be in and out of the emergency room continually to get an IV for his dehydrated body. He had been warned that he would eventually die from this. He didn't care at the time because deep down he actually had a mental illness – depression. When he finally did get help he was admitted to a local crisis unit. I don't know how he did it but when he came out for a break to smoke a cigarette he somehow got a hold of some alcohol. After he drank it, he opened the partition in the ceiling of his room there and hid the bottles. Eventually the staff found out and, in time, he did graduate from the mental health court. When I spent time talking to him, he explained some terrible traumas he had been through as a small child including watching some family members die as a result of violence.

The mental health court is so important because of the many people who are in jails and prisons who should really be in mental health facilities. It costs the state millions of dollars a year to keep these people in prison.

There was an African American woman named Mary in one our classes. Mary was one who started out behaving very tough, but I could see and hear her pain when she talked. When it was time for Mary to share her personal story, she explained that she had been a foster child and her mother abandoned her. Soon she broke out into tears as she explained that no one has ever loved her. She said she had been beaten often while growing up, and believed the reason for the beatings was simply because she was alive. When Mary spoke, I suddenly was aware of the fact that I had this strong love for her. During the breaks I talked to her, hugged her, and told her that I honestly loved her with the love of Christ. I texted her encouraging words daily, and in time she started to understand who she was and that God loved her more than she would ever know. She had believed in God for many years but had felt abandoned by Him as well as the people in her life. We have kept this strong bond to this day, and now it is Mary who texts me encouraging words!

Besides these courses we teach, the Help Hotline Community Center is open five days a week for the mentally ill to come and spend the day doing activities. There are many group homes in the area and the people usually are within walking distance of the Community Center. I have a strong love for these people and I share my time with them leading them in a <u>Masterminds: Be the Master of Your Own</u> support group. I have taught and listened, and I believe that I have learned more from them than they learn from me.

Chapter 21

Teaching in the Amish Community

A local representative from NAMI (National Alliance on Mental Illness) was working with some Amish who were mentally ill. Upon hearing this, we invited three Amish men to our class being held at Trumbull Memorial. After the first class they came up to the other teacher, Tonia, and me and asked how many children we had. We stood there speechless until we then had to admit that neither one of us had any children of our own. They looked surprised and asked "Well, then, what do you do?" I replied, "Well, we teach this class!" It soon became apparent that the one Amish gentleman wanted us to come out to his 110 acre farm where he had a large barn. There we could teach a much larger Amish group both the BRIDGES and the WRAP classes. We ended up driving out there every Tuesday night from 7 PM to 9 PM (at their request) and teaching classes in that barn.

Prior to teaching the classes, the gentleman who owned the barn asked us if we would like to make a day of coming out to visit them. So, three of us teachers, along with one teacher's wife and their two little boys, drove out there. We had a great time riding in the horse-drawn buggy, feeding the calves milk from a bottle, and seeing all the different animals they owned. We really had a good time. We took pictures and I have a photo on my wall of me driving the buggy with John, and I am holding the horse's reins. It was a little scary for me because of all the buggy accidents that have happened over the years. Sometimes the horse gets "spooked" when a car goes by and the horse runs away, or worse yet, tumbles over the side of the road. There was a little one-lane bridge on John's property, and I was sure the horse was going to fall off the bridge.

John showed us his firstborn daughter's house that he had built for them on his property when his daughter got married and had a baby. It was a very interesting house with a nice loft, and, of course, everything was made out of wood. John and his wife Jean had a beautiful home with a wood burning stove. Jean served us a delicious dinner, although we did not know what kind of meat we were eating. Their children were busy outside; one boy had gone hunting and others were jumping on a trampoline. Jean had to keep all of the food warm on the stove each day as there was no microwave to use. I was very impressed with her cooking skills and how she didn't end up burning anything.

It was obvious, as we got to know the Amish that they did live by the same principles of Christianity that we have. Jesus was born, died on a cross for our sins and healing, and rose again on the third day, which they celebrate at Easter. They have their Sunday services in different homes throughout the area instead of in a church. The Amish want to keep their traditions of living very simply and modestly in order to not be influenced by the evils of the world.

However, when a young person, girl or boy, comes of age, they can choose if they want to live in the Amish community or leave it and go out into the world and wear the regular American fashions, drive cars, live with electricity, and so on. But usually, they stay in the Amish community and marry. John had ten children who helped work the farm, and the oldest boy also worked in the concrete business with John. Each time I called John on his cell phone he was out in the fields harvesting crops or else working with concrete. John was very well known in the Amish community, particularly for his hospitality in using his barn for outside events that mainly concerned mental health. John had a strong case of bipolar disorder, and at times he would only take herbs for his illness. He could become very manic. When most of us get manic, we have "'delusions of grandeur," which usually means becoming great at something. Even so with John who would say, "I am the *best* coon hunter in the county!"

We did notice firsthand the Amish have a different standard when it comes to safety. While we were teaching WRAP one night, the children were all outside jumping on the trampoline. We heard a loud screech and soon a little boy came running into the barn to his mother. His mouth was bleeding profusely, and I stopped the class thinking this was a major crisis. Instead, the mother consoled the boy for a moment, and then told him to go out there and keep playing, as he was fine. The little boy did just that, bloody mouth and all.

We received a phone call one evening from John stating that there had been an accident. Two of his daughters were severely burned and had to go to the hospital in Cleveland. It had happened while the "young ones" were enjoying a bonfire, and every once in a while, the oldest John, Jr., would throw kerosene on the fire to keep it going. When he did this unexpectedly, two of his lovely sisters sustained burns. One of the girls was quite serious, but the other one just had first degree burns. One of the teachers assisted the family by driving them up to Cleveland and back.

The last night of teaching the Amish, we all went inside and upstairs to one of the girl's rooms as she lay in bed looking so beautiful with her long brown hair down instead of in the strict bun and bonnet. One of the teachers played her clarinet for the group and I sang "Amazing Grace." It was a heart-touching evening for all of us as we stood there close together carrying candles.

Now, to explain about the Amish who deal with mental illness, which, of course, was the group we were working with. They experience the exact same symptoms as we have, but living the way they do makes it difficult to see the symptoms. John always

182

complained that the Bishops do not understand mental illness and could give no help to someone in a deep depression. Since it was not manly to lie on the couch in mental agony for weeks at a time, John had taken to drinking alcohol to numb his mind into feeling better. Now that was precisely what someone outside of the community would do. John was a hard working ex-alcoholic and constant smoker when we met him, but he was so friendly and happy to see us each week. He told us once that "we all only go to the eighth grade, so we are looking for people who are smarter to teach us how to live better." It wasn't that we were any smarter, but that we were trained to educate people about mental illness.

The one "failing" among the Amish community is the tendency to gossip. You would think without computers they wouldn't get into all the stuff that we do, but I was actually at John and Jean's house when a young child knocked on the door with a handwritten letter he had brought from his farm informing them of something that had gone on. Therefore, when we got to the parts where they would share their personal stories, it took a while for us to ask everyone to keep the stories confidential, "under their hat," so to speak. One of the older ladies talked about trying to quit being Amish, and then going back to being Amish. Their stories were quite interesting.

So many of them had the same last names like Miller, Yoder, Byler and Hofstetler.

While we were teaching BRIDGES it happened to be winter time. The only heat in that barn was a wood burning stove, and it was absolutely freezing every week. Tonia and I began wearing ski masks when we went there. The other inconvenience was that they did not have a bathroom, but only an outhouse outside the barn. I had been locked in one for nearly an hour once in New Hampshire, so I had a bad case of PTSD when it came to that kind of bathroom. Thankfully, John would allow me to use the one in the house while carrying a candle for light.

We normally bring snacks to our classes and eat them when we take our break. Well, when working with the Amish, the ladies made wonderful snacks, like homemade pie or cookies. They also popped their own popcorn, which you would probably call "air popped" popcorn. One night I decided to fill a cup with popcorn to eat, and taking the top paper cup from a package, I filled it up with popcorn and began eating it. It wasn't long when I realized that the popcorn tasted like beer and was a bit moist the further I ate. I was concerned about this "beer instead of buttered popcorn," so I ran and told Jean about it. She said "Oh, I'm so sorry. The young boys were having a party out here earlier and they must have been drinking beer." I was a bit shocked, mainly because I hadn't had a drink myself in several years.

Chapter 22

Stability and Personal Growth

As I look back upon my life I can honestly see that there are three positive factors that have assisted me to become stable again and keep running this race called life. The first one would have to be my faith in God. I truly believe that with the Holy Spirit living in me anything is possible. Salvation, healing, love, peace and joy are all part of my daily life through meditation in the Bible and prayer. God is in the business of answering prayer and there are so many times when He intervened in my life and personally assisted me. I was not meant to commit suicide although for so many years I was sure that was the way to go. I am now "dead set" against suicide and pray for people who have fallen into that negative mind set which really is a trap. Suicide is no longer an option for me. I am happy to wait until the Lord decides my time on earth is up and then I will gladly say "Good-bye" to this life and "Hello" to eternity in heaven.

I often tell people in my classes (we have a chapter on spirituality and mental health) that the difference between a "normal" relationship with God as opposed to a manic-psychotic religious delusion is … **peace**. If it seems like God is bringing you fearful and freaky ideas about the end coming or any negative emotions or grand delusions that scare you, then you know that that is your illness manifesting. If God is bringing you peace and joy, then you know that you are experiencing the normal grace that God so freely gives. There is nothing bad that comes from God, only goodness. Sickness and disease come from Satan, although God can heal any and all diseases. Isaiah 53: 4-5 NIV states "Surely he took our infirmities and carried our sorrows, yet we considered him stricken by God, smitten by him, and afflicted. But he was pierced for our transgressions, he was crushed for our iniquities; the punishment that brought us to peace was upon him, and by his wounds we are healed." Psalm 41:3 NIV says "The Lord will sustain him on his sick bed and restore him from his bed of illness."

I love to quote scripture and pray to my Jesus any time of the day wherever I may be. To know Him is to love Him because He loves us more than we could ever imagine---*all* of us! Although I still have dealt with some depression and mania, I have never lost my faith since that day of December 15, 1991 when I gave it all up to Jesus at the altar of that old Baptist Church. "If God be for us, who can be against us?" Romans 8:31 KJV says. I'm learning that I can't concern myself with what others think of me because my goal is to please God and not people. If you are a true born-again believer in Christ you know you are going to heaven, so even in death there is life! We must *believe* what the Bible says in order to understand what it says! Once you are saved, the Bible makes sense and can assist you with any problem that may arise. It really is an individual decision. Follow Christ and live forever with Him, or deny He exists and pass away into a place called hell for eternity, a place prepared only for Satan and his followers. If you were a sex offender while on earth, then while you suffer in hell you will constantly be wanting to satisfy the craving of lust but you will never be able to. Likewise with any addiction. There is nothing that can satisfy you in hell because it is torment. The Bible says many times over that in hell "there will be weeping and gnashing of teeth." This clenching of teeth is constant because it is so impossible to bear the torture. You will also be on fire but never burn up!

I was very intrigued by a beautiful young woman's story of her descent into hell when she died. Her name is Tamara Laroux. She was in a deep depression and shot herself in the chest in a suicide attempt. As she lay curled up on the floor of her mother's bedroom, she felt her spirit leave her body, and then felt herself falling…falling into the pit of hell. When she got there, she was not depressed; she *was* depression. She was not dead she "was death," she did not have fear, she "was fear." She stated that the depression on earth was nothing compared to the depression and darkness she experienced in hell. She also was continually burning and listening to the screams of others. The main consensus of all the millions of spirits she encountered all held the same thought; "Please don't let anyone else come here." God then gave her a choice to live, and she chose life! Her wounds healed up quickly and the doctors exclaimed that it was nothing short of a miracle because the bullet from the 38 special missed her heart by ¼ of an inch. Her heart should have exploded. She wrote a book about her experiences called *Delivered*.

I love listening to sermons whether on television or at churches. After listening, I sometimes delve into the Bible myself to make sure what the preacher said was what I believe to be true also. We all need to do our very own Bible studies because the Bible is written like a love letter specifically for each of us! Because we are all unique, God wants to personally reveal to us lessons and knowledge that were written just for us to read.

People often question things that they don't understand prior to coming to the saving knowledge of our Lord Jesus Christ. For instance, how could God send anyone to hell if he loves us so much? In all actuality, it is a choice that each of us needs to make. We chose whether to accept Jesus as our Savior, or reject Him. When we ask Him to come into our lives that is when the so-called blinders are lifted from our hearts and the truth enters in and we can experience His love, peace and joy! For eternity!

It all began in the beginning, in Genesis when Eve was tempted by Satan in the form of a serpent and ate of the tree of the knowledge of good and evil. Prior to that Adam and Eve were living in a perfect world where they walked with God every day and felt comfortable living in the Garden of Eden. As soon as they ate the fruit which they were told not to, Satan had usurped the position as the "prince of this world." John 12:31 NIV, or, "the god of this age…" II Corinthians 4:4, NIV.

One of my favorite scriptures when I am feeling overwhelmed is "Peace I leave with you; my peace I give you. I do not give you as the world gives. Do not let your hearts be troubled, and do not be afraid." John 14:27, NIV.

I often have looked back at the time I spent in Butler hospital with Dr. Thomas. He was the psychiatrist who had given me the two personality disorder diagnoses. I will admit that I was in bondage back then, but now I no longer have a problem with men. I also admit that I could not keep a job back then, which was personality disorder number two. Thanks to Help Hotline, I have kept this job for over ten years. As I have read the DSM IV and saw what personality disorders were; there really were no such thing as these type of disorders as far as the "book of diagnoses " for mental disorders. They didn't even exist!

My Marriage

The second reason that I have remained stable for such long stretches of time has been because of this beautiful institution that God calls marriage. Gary and I have so much fun together, and the longer we have been married the stronger, more stable our marriage has become. Living by God's principles, Gary has gotten to the point where our conversations lean more and more on God's word and less and less on what Gary calls "Toothless Chatter." It says "Godless chatter" in the Bible but Gary just wants to make a point that nothing - truly *nothing* -is worth arguing about. It's taken a long time to get to this place but the more we pray together, study the Word together and make plans for a future of helping not only the mentally ill but those trapped in drug and alcohol addictions we feel the need to obey God in everything we do. We feel we have a call on our lives to assist these people in more of a ministry setting.

I remember from years ago, I was in one of my rants when Gary calmly said "You are too good of a person to behave this way." That was a profound statement that I will never let go of. I often *need* self-control and have learned how to *have* self-control as the years have gone past. Truly, I, in myself, could allow the behaviors of the past to rise up and become obnoxious again, but Gary and God have taught me that I AM DONE WITH THAT BEHAVIOR. As long as I live and breathe I will thank God for teaching me self-control though Gary and his calm and loving words. He is not perfect, of course, but I do believe he is perfect for me. When he and I have an entire day that we can spend together it is awesome. When we know what the Bible says, we need to obey it and believe it that arguing and complaining are sins! If that doesn't open the eyes of married couples, I don't know what would! Gary honestly tells people "I waited seven long years for my Nancy," because he had prayed for all those years for the right woman to come into his life. Although it took him a while to acknowledge it, here I am!

In 2009 Gary's mother, Dorothy, was laid to rest and after 63 years of marriage it was very difficult for Gary's Father, Frank, to get through this period of time. He moved in with us for eight months and suffered terribly with depression. I took him to a GriefShare support group every week and we helped him with every aspect of his life. His depression was relentless and although I understood it all too well, it took a long time for him to recuperate.

Thank God, Frank is now living in a beautiful assisted living and will be 92 this October. He is out of his depression and living his life by attending every Bible study and art class, going on trips to Wal-Mart and playing cards with a few of his friends every evening. We don't see him as often as we used to but talk to him on the phone every day for a "check-in." His health is remarkable for his age and he really has nothing wrong physically. We had to use his depression as the ailment to get him into the "Manor."

Gary has always been extremely close to his Dad. Gary's sister and brother all pitched in and had an Estate Sale, selling all of Dorothy's beloved furniture and everything else from the "Country Club Villa" where they had made their home. Gary's sister was very professional about this having had many successful garage sales over the years. We looked to her for prices. In just a few days we sold almost everything and what we didn't sell we divided up. Gary's sister was *very* generous with me by giving me all three closets of Dorothy's meticulously taken care of clothes and most of her jewelry along with her armoire. I am very thankful to have such a sweet sister-in-law. His brother helped out a lot with moving and carrying things during the sale, being pretty strong --like his Dad. We were very happy when the actual villa sold as well, and we got a good price for it. That all was a relief for dear Frank so that he could now move on to his "new normal." I truly think that everyone who knows Frank would agree that he is one of the kindest, sweetest, most loving men on this earth. I see that in Gary also.

Because of Frank being such a wonderful father, grandfather, and now great-grandfather, his name has been used throughout the generations. His son was named Frank, his grandson is named Frank and now he has a young great grandson named Frank.

Last year, on June 9, 2012 (our tenth wedding anniversary) Gary and I threw a huge Birthday bash here at our home for a 100th Birthday celebration as we both turned 50. There were about 120 people who came to our open house, and it was wonderful to see so many good friends and family. We had some local singers and hired a comedian all staged outdoors on the enormous deck attached to our house. We got several photos of my three sisters and myself, but not many of Gary and me as we were too busy entertaining guests. Gary and his buddy played some rock-and-roll and I think everyone had a good time. The food was catered by my sister Chris Brown's sister-in-law who only charged us for the food which she then prepared. Everyone said the food was excellent and there wasn't much left the next day! We also had a chocolate fountain with all sorts of fruit, graham crackers, vanilla wafers and anything else you could think of to dip chocolate in. Although we said "no gifts" on the invitation we received a lot of cards with money and some really funny "old" jokes too. It was definitely another memorable party that was nothing but a good time. (I was secretly celebrating deep inside that I had not committed suicide and was able to celebrate my 50th birthday…I had come so close so many times). Praise God!

Career

Last but certainly not least, my third saving grace has been working at Help Hotline. It will be 13 years ago this December when I enjoyed my first day of work by leading a huge group of the mental health consumers in Christmas Carols at the NAMI (National Alliance on Mental Illness) Christmas Party. What a first day of work! Although I tried to quit a few times—strictly because "old habits are hard to break"— I thank God that the folks at Help Hotline did not give up on me. I was and am still honored to be a part of the Help Hotline family. While I was suffering through those years of dark days and suicidal nights, I *never* would have thought that one day I would be considered an inspiration to others suffering from mental illness, (at least that is what I have been told).

What I do at Help Hotline is very minimal in comparison to all the programs Help Hotline offers to the community. Not only does the trained staff answer approximately 18,000 calls a month from the crisis hotline which is available 24/7, they also offer another alternative, the Warm Line that people with mental health issues can call, and a trained "peer"—someone who has also suffered with a mental illness—will answer to assist the person.

In 2003 the Help Hotline building itself was doubled in size under the direction of Duane Piccirilli and the Board. In 2006, the local Mental Health Board and Help Hotline purchased a beautiful building called "The Community Center" or "Drop-In Center" for all the mentally ill consumers to come to each day and do activities (as mentioned before). The building used to be a library and has a nice conference room where many meetings are held, including mental health courses as well.

Help Hotline provides a Payeeship Program which assists people with mental health diagnoses in paying their bills and keeping account of their money. During the winter months, Help Hotline has a Cold Weather Emergency Shelter Program which helps in transporting homeless people to the Mahoning Valley Rescue Mission to get a good night's sleep.

They also have an Intensive Guardian Program. This program authorizes licensed social workers who basically "take on" responsibility for the lives of people with severe mental illness who cannot take care of themselves. The guardian makes decisions regarding where the person lives, when they need something, or need to go into the hospital.

Help Hotline also assists the mentally ill with housing through the Mahoning County Housing Opportunities (MCHOP).The PATH (Project for Assistance in Transition from Homelessness) provides outreach to the homeless population in Mahoning and Trumbull Counties. There are staff members who work in this program who have experienced mental illness and may have been homeless themselves at some point.

The agency is involved in a Tri-County Family Violence Prevention Coalition along with a Victims Assistance Program and a Victims of Crime Support Service. There is also a program for

Special Needs Children whose criteria is for developmentally disabled children from birth to age 21.

Because of my association with Help Hotline I have had many opportunities that I would not have had otherwise, and I appreciate the people there more than they could ever know.

During my tenure at Help Hotline there have been more than ten teachers trained to assist in teaching the BRIDGES course, having received the full week training at Dayton, Ohio. Since OAMH dissolved I have been given that task and have trained four more. All in all, I believe that we have taught over 1,000 students the course since its inception.

We began facilitating WRAP courses with training ten teachers in 2007, and have taught nearly 25 courses so far in Trumbull and Mahoning counties.

After reading many evaluations in both counties, it is so refreshing to see how these classes have influenced and continue to change many lives for the better.

In 2011 Help Hotline nominated me for an award from the Margaret Clark Morgan Foundation. My sister, Chris, who had watched helplessly as I suffered from mental illness for years and could not help me, thought this foundation was a good match for Help Hotline, and in turn, would help our program. I gave the website to Duane, years ago, and thus we began our funding by The Margaret Clark Morgan Foundation. When I received a letter from the Foundation in 2011, stating that I won the Impact Award for Transformation, I was surprised and humbled! A camera crew came to The Community Center and filmed me teaching my class, and then interviewed several people who had taken the classes or had become teachers. It was all good, but stressful at the same time! The night of the banquet in November of 2011 a short clip of my work was shown, and then I was called up to receive the award. It was a night I will never forget. We had a large table filled with many of my favorite people, including my therapist and two of my sisters, my brother-in-law, Keith, along with my father and father-in-law. (My mother couldn't make it due to health issues.) Duane was there too, pretending he had nothing to do with me winning this award when he himself had asked me for a bio.

In May of 2013 Duane asked me to be the keynote speaker at the Community Counseling Center's annual dinner in Hermitage, Pennsylvania. I invited my sister, Chris, and she was a great support to have there. Again, I wrote a speech and practiced it many times. I even went as far as tape recording it while outside on my deck, then listening to it over and over as the birds chirped, dogs barked, and the local church bells chimed, all caught on tape.

Duane had arranged to have the reporter from the local newspaper interview me afterward. He actually asked for a copy of my speech and I gave it to him, thereby putting the "meat and potatoes" of the speech right there in the newspaper. The next day I was teaching my version of <u>Masterminds: Be the Master of Your Own</u> for a group of mental health consumers there at the counseling center. Again, the reporter showed up afterward and interviewed me and took some photos.

My association with Help Hotline is very important to me, most of all because of the many people I have met who are dealing with mental illness and/or substance abuse problems, who I am able to touch and encourage and help them live more stable and meaningful lives. I have come to love and respect these people who suffer emotionally, and if this book has helped even one more person who is living through this tough journey, then my task was worthwhile.

Epilogue

My parents, Joan and Stewart McCurdy are still living in the house we grew up in Cortland. I will do anything to help them in their older years. They have done so much for me. THAT list is endless! Now in July of 2019 they are doing very well for our mother being 88 and our father who will be 91 this month. We had a lovely 80th Birthday party/Easter celebration at a local restaurant for my mother and our entire family made the effort to be there. We also celebrated her 88th birthday with an Easter/Birthday family party. There are many cherished times to remember.

Gary's father, Frank passed away at the age of 93 on April 1, 2016.

My family has watched me suffer the torment of mental illness. I could not hide it from them. There was a time when some of them were convinced that I was going to commit suicide and began distancing themselves from me so that it would not be so unbearable when it happened. This is what I have been told. As mentioned throughout this book, I, myself, was positive that I would die by my own hand. The grip of depression no longer haunts me, nor do I embrace it. I have made my decision to live. If you or anyone in your family is thinking of ending your life please remember: the thoughts are temporary, the act of suicide is permanent. Get help from a professional, take medication if you need to, but never, never, never give in to those negative thoughts or voices! Invariably, there is something wonderful in store for you right around the corner! If you have had a bad experience going to a church and being ostracized by people in any way, remember, they are only people who have no understanding of what you are going through or what you may need. Try another church until you find one that the people are

195

welcoming and filled with love. There are many positive groups you can join. Take a look at the World Wide Web and find a local group near you that deals with mental illness and/or substance abuse.

I also volunteer at The Mahoning Valley HOPE Center located in Warren. I facilitate my group <u>Masterminds: Be the Master of Your Own</u> once a week with the intent to assist others with mental illnesses and substance abuse problems to live their lives with dignity and hope. Gary and I also attend Victory Christian Center and also attend North-Mar church.

In 2015, I made the decision to leave my employment at the Help Network of Northeast Ohio (formerly Help Hotline Crisis Center, Inc.) I am now employed by a large mental health agency in Ohio and I work as a Certified Peer Recovery Specialist.

Last but not least, remember the God who created you. He will never let you down. He is always there. He is just waiting for you to acknowledge Him.

Blessings and Love to you today and always!

www.ingramcontent.com/pod-product-compliance
Lightning Source LLC
Chambersburg PA
CBHW070901290526
45795CB00001B/195